Toward a Common Hope

Toward a Common Hope

Chautauqua Lake Sermons

ROBERT ALLAN HILL

WIPF & STOCK · Eugene, Oregon

TOWARD A COMMON HOPE
Chautauqua Lake Sermons

Wipf & Stock
An Imprint of Wipf and Stock Publishers
199 W. 8th Ave., Suite 3
Eugene, OR 97401

www.wipfandstock.com

PAPERBACK ISBN: 978-1-5326-5741-2
HARDCOVER ISBN: 978-1-5326-5742-9
EBOOK ISBN: 978-1-5326-5743-6

Manufactured in the U.S.A.   10/25/18

Contents

Preface

In August of 2017, Jan and I had the privilege of enjoying the unique setting, surroundings, program, and leadership of The Chautauqua Institution. From August 6th to 13th, we were engaged in the music, lectures, discussions, dinners, and informal conversations which make Chautauqua such a unique and powerful means and mode of grace, summer by summer. This book of sermons collects those preached in that week (the first six), along with others that had been brought along in reserve (the last five), as it were, in case they were needed.

The Spaniards have a term and tradition to identify a form of ongoing, lengthy, easy conversation which is somewhat harder to come by here in America—*una tertulia*—an engaged and engaging conversation. Chautauqua, though ruggedly American, rural not urban, still historically Methodist, and altogether different from the *paseos* and taverns of Madrid, Segovia, or Barcelona, does share the same regard (even reverence) for conversation. We would like to thank those friends, old and new, with whom we spoke at Chautauqua, for their heart, mind, and spirit, generously shared on the porches, along the lakeside, over dinner, and on the walkways of the Institution, which is so precious and unique to New York and to the United States.

In particular, we express our thanks for the warm hospitality and unstinting kindness of Chautauqua's leaders, including but not limited to President Michael Hill; Department of Religion Director, the Rev. Dr. Robert Franklin: and Department of Religion

PREFACE

Associate Director (now in fact director herself), Ms. Maureen Rovegno.

In the evenings, walking on the bank of the Charles River in Boston, something of the spirit of Chautauqua strides along with us, week by week, and a shimmering reminder of learning harnessed to piety, a glimpse of what gracious life can be, and the tunes and words of sacred hymns meant for singing in the warm open summer air: *Now on land and sea descending brings the night its peace profound; let our vesper hymn be blending with the holy calm around; Jubilate! Jubilate! Jubilate! Amen; let our vesper hymn be blending with the holy calm around.*

The Rev. Dr. Robert Allan Hill
Dean, Marsh Chapel
Professor, New Testament and Pastoral Theology
Chaplain to the University, Office of Religious Life
Boston University
6173583394
rahill@bu.edu

The Sermon on the Mound

Galatians 5:1

Sunday, August 6th, 2017

Out on the Massachusetts Bay, in the autumn of 1630, Governor Jonathan Winthrop spoke to frightened pilgrims, half of whom would be dead before spring. One can try to imagine the rolling of the frigate in the surf, out on the Atlantic. One can feel the salt breeze, the water wind of the sea. The Governor is brief, in his sermon for the day: "We must consider that we shall be a city upon a hill. The eyes of all people are upon us, so that if we shall deal falsely with our God in this work we have undertaken, and so cause Him to withdraw His present help from us, we shall be made a story and a byword through the world."[1] A remarkable, truly remarkable warning to our country at the moment of its inception.

It is a cold day in early March, 1865. Four score and eight years after Independence, the nation has indeed become, as Winthrop prophesied in his Boston sermon, "a story and byword through the world." 600,000 men will have died by the time Lee and Grant meet at Appomattox, approximately one death for every 10 slaves forcibly brought to the New World. This day in March, Mr. Lincoln delivers his own sermon, to the gathered and—we may assume—chastened congress. It is Lincoln's Second Inaugural address:

---

1. Winthrop, "Model of Christian Charity," 246.

The Almighty has His own purposes . . . Fondly do we hope, fervently do we pray, that this mighty scourge of war may speedily pass away. Yet, if God wills that it continue until all the wealth piled by the bondsman's two hundred and fifty years of unrequited toil shall be sunk, and until every drop of blood drawn with the lash shall be paid by another drawn with the sword, as was said three thousand years ago, so still it must be said, "The judgments of the Lord are true and righteous altogether."

With malice toward none, with charity for all, with firmness in the right as God gives us to see the right, let us strive on to finish the work that we are in, to bind up the nation's wounds, to care for him who shall have borne the battle and for his widow and his orphan, to do all which may achieve and cherish a just and lasting peace among ourselves and with all nations.[2]

Into the next decade, the state of Mississippi will spend 20 percent of its annual budget, each year, for artificial limbs. Lincoln himself will die within weeks.

Now we witness another gathering, and we hear another sermon. A hundred more years have passed. It is August 28th, 1963, a sweltering day in the nation's capital. Hundreds of thousands of women and men have gathered within earshot of Lincoln's memorial and within earshot of his Second Inaugural. They have come—maybe some of you were there—with firmness in the right as God gives to see the right, to strive to finish the work. A Baptist preacher captures the moment in ringing oratory: "I have a dream that one day, on the red hills of Georgia, the sons of former slaves and the sons of former slave-owners will be able to sit down at the table of brotherhood."[3]

Winthrop. Lincoln. King. 1630. 1865. 1963. These are the three greatest sermons ever preached in our country's history. Do you notice that not one of them was delivered in a church? Yet they all interpret the church's Gospel to the land of the free and the home of the brave.

2. Lincoln, "Second Inaugural Address," 477.
3. King Jr., "Speech at Civil Rights March," 823.

Winthrop. Lincoln. King. They believed in God's providence. They trusted, through terror, in God's favor. They thought that persons, that even they themselves, had roles to play in the divine drama. They warned of tragedy, they endured tragedy, and they honestly acknowledged tragedy. What Winthrop prophesied, what Lincoln witnessed, and what King attacked is our national tragedy still. We still judge by the color of skin and not by the content of character. And now, in this year of our Lord 2017, we see across the land a shredding of inherited forms of civil society on a weekly basis, a shredding of healthy culture, a shredding of respect for language, rhetoric, and speech—tweet by tweet by blessed tweet.

But God has not left us nor does God abandon God's children. God works through human hearts to bind up the nation's wounds. It is the preaching of the Gospel of Jesus Christ, and this alone, which will bring peace. The church has nothing better to do, nothing other to do, nothing more important to do, and nothing else to do than to preach. Preaching is everything, the whole nine yards. Let others be anxious and fretful over much service: you are a Christian—sit at Christ's feet and lisp his Gospel to others. For when the Gospel is rightly preached and rightly heard, heaven invades earth.

We await a common hope. We await a faith amenable to culture and a culture amenable to faith. We await a fierce combination of a deep personal faith and an active social involvement. We await the will power to *do all the good we can, at all the times we can*. We await Christ not just against culture, not just in culture, not just above culture, and not just in paradox with culture—but Christ transforming culture!

The best preaching happens beyond church. Some is spoken and some is lived. Said Benjamin Franklin, teaching the only two values he thought important—industry and frugality: "None preaches better than the ant, and he says nothing."[4] We are not so much resident aliens as dual citizens.

We have no choice about common identity, national character, love of country. Listen to Winthrop and Lincoln and King.

---

4. Franklin, "Poor Richard's Almanac, 1735," 319.

What we have some limited influence over is the nature, the type, the relative health of such. Notice the Beatitudes, how the blessing fall on groups. Blessed are those . . .

I believe there is at least one saving story from which, over time, we may gain strength and insight for our common story, poetry and preaching. What Whitman said about poetry is doubly true for the Gospel itself:

> The United States themselves are essentially the greatest poem . . . Here, at last, is something in the doings of man that corresponds with the broadcast doings of the day and the night . . . Really great poetry is always the result of a national spirit, and not the privilege of a polished and select few the strongest and sweetest songs yet remain to be sung.[5]

Here is what a godly love of country can do.

This year, without much fanfare, we passed the seventieth anniversary of Jackie Robinson's entrance into major league baseball. The armed forces were still legally segregated. So were public schools. That was America in 1947, when a tee-totaling, Bible-quoting Republican from Ohio integrated major league baseball. Who remembers today the lone ranger type—so decried in church circles today—who spent most of a lifetime working for one transformation. Rickey was taught the Gospel in the Methodist church of that time where there was to be no separation, like that we have today, between a deep personal faith (conservative) and an active social involvement (liberal). Rickey was one of those people who just never heard that "it can't be done." For thirty years, slowly and painstakingly, he maneuvered and strategized and planned and brought about the greatest change in the history of our national pastime. *It can be done.* Go to Cooperstown this summer and see the story unfold. There is sermon on the mound, preached in life, brought to voice through one lone Methodist, in one lone lifetime, in one lone sport, in one lone generation. *It can be done.* But you

5. Whitman, "Leaves of Grass," 519.

need a preacher, like Rickey: "I prefer the errors of enthusiasm to the reticence of wisdom."[6]

- Where is the Branch Rickey of Wall Street?
- Where is the Branch Rickey of the local church?
- Where is the Branch Rickey of the public school?
- Where is the Branch Rickey of your neighborhood?
- Where is that secular saint who doesn't realize it can't be done?
- Where is the preacher of the next sermon on the mound?
- Maybe she is here today. Maybe you are she.

I heard William McClain, an African-American preacher, tell about growing up in Tuskegee, Alabama. He grew up listening to the team Branch Rickey fielded in Brooklyn. "When Jackie stood at the plate, we stood with him. When he struck out, we did too. When he hit the ball, we jumped and cheered. When he slid home, we dusted off our own pants. When he stole a base, he stole for us. When he hit a home run, we were the victors. And when he was spiked, we felt it, a long way away, down south. He gave us hope. He gave us hope."[7]

Don't let people tell you things can't change for the better. They can. This country can work. We just need a few more Branch Rickeys and a few sermons on the mound.

For freedom, Christ has set us free. Stand fast, therefore, and do not be enslaved again.

6. Rickey, "Branch Rickey Quotes."

7. From the author's memory, during a sermon at UMCNCNY Annual Conference in 1995.

Marks of the New Age

Luke 24:1-12

1 Corinthians 15:19-26

Monday, August 7th, 2017

Opening: Canadian Creed

Our Gospel provides a particular kind of memory, a powerful kind of prayer, and a persistent kind of love as hallmarks of hope. Do they mark your life? Do memory (*remember how he told you . . . and they remembered his words*), prayer (*they bowed their faces to the ground*), and love (*they went to the tomb, taking the spices which they had prepared*) clothe life for you?

On Easter morning, women with courage walked tomb-ward to work through their worst experience. They set forth to do the work of facing grief with grace, failure with faith, hurt with hope, and death with dignity. And thee? Is that work begun, continued, or completed? Easter brings you life, uplifts, a lift for living, even into the teeth of death, so you may face, face down, and live down death.

Death makes us mortal. Facing death makes us human.

God is at work in the world to make and keep human life human.

The Gospel means to uplift you, to fill you with a common hope—listen, hear, trust—from death to life. Seek "the Living One," he who is more alive than all life, whose life is the marrow of being alive. Why do you seek the Living One (*ton zonta*)—a title perhaps, a Person, for sure, an announcement of Christ, crucified and risen. All appearances to the contrary notwithstanding:

> The marks of the new age are present hidden in the old age. At the juncture of the ages, the marks of the resurrection are hidden and revealed in the cross of the disciple's daily death, and only there . . . this is what the turn of the ages means, that life is manifested in death.[1]

We need not over-preach, even at Chautauqua. We still walk by faith, not by sight. We still see in a mirror, dimly. We still have this treasure in earthen vessels. We still hope for what we do not see. The resurrection follows but does not replace the cross.

Paul? "Paul gives no indication that he is familiar with the doctrine of the empty tomb. There is not the remotest reference to it in any of his letters, and his conviction that the resurrection body is not the body of this flesh but a spiritual body waiting for the soul of man in heaven makes it improbable that he would have found it congenial."[2]

The Gospel comes with the morning, every morning. So walk with the women and walk with me too. Let us walk together through the Gospel in sermon. And if you get done with the sermon before the sermon gets done—if you are finished with it before I am—have no fear, do not worry. Just wait a bit, and I will catch up with you! And fear not, some of you will arise inspired and some will awake refreshed, and both outcomes are worthy!

Marathon 2013

We do not know what a day will bring. This is true of every day, but truer of some days than others. Focus for a moment on the *gravest* of days you have known. Someday I would like to hear of it.

For some whom we know well, Patriots' Day 2013 was such a day, nearly 3 years ago. We learned first-hand in this neighborhood about the visitation of death, tragically known again in Brussels

---

1. Martyn, "Epistemology," 273.
2. Gilmour, *Gospel According to St. Luke*, 416.

and around the globe this week. Spelled D-E-A-T-H. Not your imaginary friend, but an equally omnipresent invisible enemy.

That Monday began with brunch and celebration, but ended with terror, needless slaughter, and (humanly speaking) unforgivable horror. Our staff opened the chapel later for the throngs walking, T-less, by. Water, refreshment, prayer, counsel, they gave. One runner came very cold and was shrouded with a clergy gown—all we had to offer, a shepherd's outfit. What a week. Tuesday brought us to the plaza, come evening, in vigil, to honor and reflect. Wednesday, in this chapel, and also at other hours in other settings, gathered us for ordered worship, prayer, music, liturgy, Eucharist, and sermon. Thursday, we heard President Obama, on a familiar theme, "running the race set before us." Friday, at home, we watched the televised news. Saturday, we listened for the musical succor of Handel's beautiful *Messiah*, right here. The next Monday, we gathered again for a memorial service, for our deceased Boston University student, Lu Lingzi.

Death makes us mortal. Facing death makes us human.

You remember death. Your neighbor. Your hourly companion. You spell his or her name D-E-A-T-H. Easter morning is about intimations of life, the Living One outlasting death. Paul: *as in Adam, all die, so also in Christ shall all be made alive* (1 Cor 15:22). Behold: a glimmer of light in the dark, a rumor of life in death, an angel reclining in the tomb.

Clem: Memory

Memory gives us life. *Remember how he told you . . .*

If there has been ever an age that needed better memory more than ours, I know not what it would have been. *Those who do not remember history are doomed to repeat it.*[3] *The past is not dead; it is not even past.*[4]

---

3. Santayana, "Life of Reason," 629.

4. Wikipedia, "Requiem for a Nun."

During that week, journalists from around the globe contacted us and others across the university. Many, perhaps most, called or wrote from Asia. Some needed commentary for radio news or other newscasts. The main newspapers across the country also sent reporters.

On Wednesday, the office took a call from the *Philadelphia Enquirer*. Could someone meet their man and his photographer at the steps of the chapel to help convey something of the nightly vigils, services, and informal prayers of the week. We picked a mid-afternoon hour. In the April sunlight, the interview began. Suddenly, the photographer dropped his camera and shouted: "Bob. Bob. Bob!" His name is Clem Murray, a high school classmate and friend. He and his girlfriend Mimi Sinopoli were the "class couple" because they were the most beautiful couple, a truly stunning two-some. I had seen neither of them for forty years. I had heard that they married in college. Somehow, he recognized enough of my former self, hidden behind the current condition of my condition, and recognized my name. He let go of the camera for a hug. We finished the interview and photo. I turned then, as they were going to ask, "So how is Mimi?" You only know the really awkward moments too late. They come up after you, like alligators out of the Florida swamp. Clem said nothing. He didn't need to. I could see what he was holding back in his face and eyes. He just shook his head and shook. "Two years ago, she died of cancer." In the midst of life, we are in death, at every moment. All I could see of her was a white graduation gown, a little cap and tassel. Three decades of marriage, three children, all things bright and beautiful, and then a malignancy unto death. Clem waved goodbye. A kairos, not a chronos moment.

We held, together, a memory of life that made life, that gave life, that made alive. In the very presence of death. It was a resurrection memory. A living memory takes you out of the present and into a living past. It was a resurrection memory. And perhaps the most powerful personal conversation I have known.

With his madeleine moment, Marcel Proust teaches us best: "A single minute released from the chronological order of time has re-created in us the human being similarly released . . . situated outside the scope of time, what could one fear from the future . . . (these are) resurrections of the past."[5]

Memory gives us life.

Ceremonial Bow: Prayer

Prayer gives us life.

A week after the Marathon, we memorialized our student, Lu Lingzi. This service was held, as had been the memorial for President John Silber the autumn before, in the George Sherman Union. Two thousand attended, with an unknown number around the globe watching and listening by cybercast. The service proceeded, word and music, after careful attention and planning by musicians and clergy. We heard the Gospel of Mark and the Analects of Confucius. We listened to instrumental and choral music. We grieved, remembered, accepted, and affirmed together. The family, eighteen or so, dressed in black and sat in the front row. As the service ended, from the next row, I could see and hear a susurration along the family pew. They were meant to move to the gathering and greeting room, but no one stood. Further conversation moved up and down the row in a language I could of course not understand. I feared: have we forgotten a eulogy, left out a reading, or skipped over an anthem? No. It was something else. After a moment, the family, dressed in black, stood as one, moved as one, turned as one, and faced the congregation and the world. A long quiet ensued. Then, as one, they bowed at the waist and held the bow. To honor the gathering, to honor the moment, to honor the life, to honor Life, they bowed, in silence. It was a resurrection prayer. And it is perhaps the most powerful liturgical moment I have ever known.

"Different are the languages of prayer, but the tears are all the same."[6] We should repeat this three times a day.

---

5. Proust, *Remembrance of Things Past*, 2:992–96.

6. Schulweis, "Two Prophets, One Soul."

Prayer gives us life.

Hold On: Love

Love gives us life. *They went to the tomb . . .*

The next Sunday, April 28th, turned out to be a nice, warm, early-spring day. As the sun came up, we looked forward to a day of rest and worship and a chance for a return to normal.

About one hour before the Sunday service, Br. Larry came in to the office to say, "We have another one." It took me some moments to understand and internalize the fact of another death. She had died tragically in a fire, caught in an upper room. Her mother would be coming up from New York City on the bus later that evening. The police would have informed her of her daughter's death. Our Dean of Students, Kenn Elmore, his associate, John Battaglino, and I planned to meet the bus. That evening, we awaited a delayed Greyhound, talking a bit about the week past. We pondered how best to greet the grieving mom. It was decided I would meet the bus and greet her as she came down the steps, offer our heartfelt condolences, and start the trek over to the hotel. The noise of the terminal, the lateness of the hour, the long weeks of terror and loss, and the approximate presence of death itself settled on us, giving us that quiet of the soul that sometimes overtakes us.

In the bus rolled. The mother came down the steps carrying a beautifully decorated box, holding it with both hands.

"I want to greet you for the University and express our deepest sympathy and heartfelt concern" I said.

"Where is my daughter?" she replied, "What hospital is she in? Please take me to her so I can see her and talk with her. I want to go and see her. Where is she? How is she doing? I brought a rice cake. See. In the box. It is her favorite. Rice cake. I know it will make her feel better."

Honestly, at every phrase, I tried to say, with honesty and kindness, that her daughter had in fact died the night before, caught in an awful fire. Apparently, she did not understand the police, they did not speak clearly, or someone else in the family took the call. I tried everything. But she could not understand or could not hear, until, at last, she looked up and asked, "You mean . . . she . . . is dead?" Yes. There is a phrase in the Christmas gospel about Rachel weeping for her children. That Bus Terminal echoed with the chilling, haunting, and painful cries of a mother who rightly could not and would not be consoled, as Rachel could not. The reverberation of her sobbing across that urban nighttime cacophony I can hear still. Nothing I said helped. Nothing I did helped. Nothing I could offer her could she receive. We sat on a bench, the wailing stronger still, the cake and box on the floor, the gathered friends lost in grief. Then, she stiffened, her arm becoming taut and cold in mine. Perhaps she was going into shock. Everything I tried—counsel, prayer, listening, scripture—all was of no avail.

Then, from her other side, Dean Elmore simply surrounded and enfolded her. He put all of his body and arms around her as she wailed and stiffened. He held her. He rocked her. He embraced her. And little by little, sob by sob, she began to relax. And little by little, breath by breath, she began to loosen up. And little by little, held tight, she came through it. Her lament lessened, her limbs loosened. Out up from the tomb she came. A physical, unspoken compassion brought her through, from death to life. It was a resurrection love, compassion, embrace, grace, freedom, care, acceptance, mercy, pardon, peace, inclusion. It was a resurrection love. And it is perhaps the most powerful, public, pastoral ministry I have witnessed.

Unamuno: *warmth, warmth, warmth; we are dying of cold not of darkness; it is not the night that kills, it is the frost.*[7]

Six years ago, at the time of our dad's death, Elie Wiesel sent a note. It was love physical, compassionate, and personal, and, as with all resurrection love, it made a difference. It concluded: *we have a saying in our tradition, "may you be spared another further hardship."*

Love gives us life.

Memory. Prayer. Love.

7. See Unamuno, "Tragic Sense of Life," 631.

The marks of the new age are present hidden in the old age. At the juncture of the ages, the marks of the resurrection are hidden and revealed in the cross of the disciple's daily death, and only there . . . this is what the turn of the ages means, that life is manifested in death.[8]

Hear the Gospel: memory, prayer, love, creation, redemption, sanctification, Father, Son, Spirit, and life in death. Life in death holds out a promise of something grander still, life after death.

Closing: Apostles Creed

8. Martyn, "Epistemology," 273.

Exit or Voice?

Philippians 1:21
Tuesday, August 8th, 2017
For me to live is Christ and to die is gain.

Frontispiece

Over pasta last summer, on a hot July night, six of us of long friendship ate and talked. For decades, our dear friend has been a committed participant in a community group. She has taken pride in her work, preparing and practicing for her role, recruiting others and helping in the community. With spaghetti, wine, and the warmth of long relationship, we nodded and supped. But something had happened. The old committee chair left. A new one came. He was, sadly, rude and belligerent with his helpers. Not just once or twice.

Said she: "What should I do? I love the group, and I love my team. But his behavior I cannot abide. I have talked to him. He rebuffs me. If I stay, I endure and even collude in his misbehavior, but I will still have my voice in the group and with the committee. If I leave, I exit from what I love and also leave behind any influence I might have to help, support, or protect others. I am loyal to my friends, but I am ready to go. What should I do?"

Hours, days, and months are actually shot through with this form of dilemma in choice. Exit or voice? A famous study, written at MIT forty-five years ago, laid out for economists the dimensions of the dilemma.[1] But such a condition goes well beyond the marketplace.

Having introduced our gospel, let us re-introduce ourselves, one to another . . .

We are grateful for your witness here, at Chautauqua, your ubiquitous ministry—lay, musical, clerical, and all. Incidentally, Peter Gomes left us a clue or two about ministry:

> You ask me the secret of my success in ministry at Harvard over forty years? I give it to you in a single word: ubiquity. I am everywhere. I go everywhere. I attend everything. I enter every building and dorm. I walk through every yard and hill and valley and molehill. I go where I am invited. I go where I am not invited. I go where I am expected. I go where I am not expected. Surprise! It's me. You ask my secret? I give it to you in a word: ubiquity. I am ubiquitous.[2]

Both exit and voice are themselves ubiquitous. Exit is as old as the exit from the Garden of Eden. Voice is as old as the dominical voice of Christ resisting temptation. Exit and voice: how do our Scriptures help us frame such living choices? These are good Lenten meditations. Paul: For me, to live is Christ—voice—to die is gain—exit.

Paul longs for exit. Paul lives for voice.

Student Life

Students of every age and stage—after all, we are all disciples, are we not?—understand the strange interplay between trial and faith. But that understanding comes through the ministry, here, of Asbury First, your location, history, architecture, program, music, pastoral care, and, especially, your voice. Good thing. In a recent *Atlantic* article, Marshall Poe concludes his essay:

1. See Hirschman, *Exit, Voice, and Loyalty.*
2. In conversation with the author, 2009.

American higher education is the envy of the world. Students come here from all over the globe to study. And American higher education is something we, as citizens, should be very proud of, for we built and fund a large portion of it. It's really one of our crowning achievements as a nation.

American higher education has, however, one glaring deficiency: it does not teach its undergraduates how to live. It teaches them when the French Revolution was, what the carbon cycle is, and how to solve for X. It does not teach them what to do when they feel confused, alone, and scared. When they break down after a break-up. When they are so depressed they cannot get out of bed. When they drink themselves into unconsciousness every night. When they find themselves living on someone's couch. When they decide to go off their meds. When they flunk a class or even flunk out of school. When they get fired. When a sibling dies. When they don't make the team. When they get pregnant. When their divorced parents just won't stop fighting. When they are too sick to get to the hospital. When they lose their scholarship. When they've been arrested for vandalism. When they hate themselves so much that they begin self-mutilating. When they're thinking about suicide. When they force themselves to throw up after every meal. When they turn to drugs for relief from their pain. When they've been assaulted or raped. When their mind is racing and cannot stop. When they wonder about the meaning of it all. When they are terrified by the question, "What do I do next?"[3]

Philippians

How shall we use our human freedom faithfully in the light of the divine freedom known to us in Christ? We return to our Scripture and explore our experience. For this, the witness of the church—Asbury First—is crucial.

---

3. Poe, "Colleges Should Teach Religion."

How beloved are the golden verses of Philippians. I propose that a survey of favorite verses—not your favorite hymn, psalm, or parable, but your single favorite verse—would show a heavy reliance on Philippians:

> I thank my God in every remembrance of you. (Phil 1:3)
>
> Thankful for your partnership in the gospel from the first day until now. (Phil 1:5)
>
> For me to live is Christ and to die is gain. (Phil 1:21)
>
> If there is any encouragement in Christ, any incentive of love, any participation in the Spirit, be of that mind. (Phil 2:1)
>
> Have that mind among yourselves which you have in Christ Jesus, who took the form of a servant. (Phil 2:5)
>
> That at the name of Jesus every knee should bow, in heaven and on earth and under the earth, and every tongue confess that Jesus Christ is Lord, to the glory of God the Father. (Phil 2:10–11)
>
> Forgetting what lies behind and straining forward to what lies ahead, I press on toward the goal for the prize of the upward call of God in Christ Jesus. (Phil 3:13)
>
> Our commonwealth is in heaven, and from it we await a savior. Rejoice in the Lord always, again I say, rejoice. (Phil 4:4)
>
> Have no anxiety about anything, but in all things by prayer and supplication with thanksgiving let your requests be made known to God. (Phil 4:6)
>
> Whatever is true, honorable, just, pure, lovely, gracious, excellent, praiseworthy, think about these things. (Phil 4:8)
>
> I know how to be abased and I know how to abound. . . . I can do all things in him who strengthens me. (Phil 4:12)

Experience

Take heart for the long journey, the daily exit from the green garden, and the hourly summons of the dominical voice. The strange world of the Bible nourishes us.

Exit or voice—or resignation? Fight or flight—or play dead?

Your roommate smokes for breakfast, drugs for lunch, drinks for dinner. Do you leave—him, school, or both? Do you confront—"one of us is crazy and I think it's you"? Do you grin and bear it? Your faculty has taken a new direction, that is, a wrong turn. For well-intentioned reasons, in the plan for a new curriculum, they have exchanged birthright for pottage. Do you politic, agitate, criticize, and combat in what may well be a losing cause? Do you call a friend who has wanted you to come to Cornell or Colgate for a long time anyway and prepare to exit? Or do you close your door, grade your papers, and play a little more golf?

You are a young person entering ministry and a cradle Methodist. You affirm the full humanity of gay people and eschew any bigotry against sexual minorities. Do you exit and seek orders in the Lutheran, Presbyterian, Episcopalian, Congregational, American Baptist, or Unitarian churches? Or do you stay and lift your voice within Methodism, recognizing that the struggle will be generational in length (longer than my lifetime, perhaps), global in breadth (requiring the warming and freeing of African hearts and votes), and gritty in depth (underground railways to marry gays and deploy ordained gays—both prayer and political love.)

Your brother is about to marry the wrong woman. He is impressionable and she is impressive—an empress if you will. Do you shout a warning and then risk never speaking to him again? Do you reason, consult, have lunch, empathize, and appeal to the better angels of his nature? Do you throw up your hands, send an early shower gift, and bite your tongue?

You are a major world superpower. With limited success, you have partially pacified a part of the Middle East. Now what? Do you exit stage left, leaving behind a decade of warfare, tens of thousands dead, tribal hatreds still much in evidence, and hope for the best? Do you stay, increase your footprint and military presence, giving voice to the rights and needs of children, women, nonmuslims, and others? Or do you practice a little benign neglect, and put your energy into health care, immigration reform, nuclear disarmament, Chinese economics, and the next election?

You are the dad in an immigrant family where three have papers and two do not. Do you stay, with risk, placing your voice in chorus with that of Emma Lazarus ("Give me your tired, your poor . . ."), or do you exit, to Montreal, to the Olympic Stadium, and make a new life?

You are a member of a nearby city church, which is about to be closed by superintendents, general and district, neither of whom has ever served a city church in upstate New York. What do you do? Go down the street? Write a letter? Exit or voice?

You are on your third session of marriage counseling. You know that, "I do," cannot become, "I redo." But you need some growing space. What do you do?

You are a great, large church in a shrinking, splintering denomination. Your buildings, savings, endowments, and apportionments are held in trust for the denomination. Your ministerial leadership comes thence by appointment. How do you address this relationship? With distance, silence, absence, and exit, hoping for the best? Or with proximity, noise, presence, and voice, planning for the worst?

Today's Lesson

How much for exit and how much for voice? How much for flight and how much for fight? And then, when do you just pull your turtle head back into the shell and play dead?

In 54 AD, Paul of Tarsus, the Apostle to the Gentiles, in a verse with links to exit and voice, wrestled with the same angel/demon.

On one hand, he wrote: "For me, to live is Christ, to die is gain. Yet which I shall choose I cannot tell" (Phil 1:21). For once, his regular apocalyptic eschatology, the horizontal primitive hope of the day of the Lord, which he fully expects to see in the flesh, gives way to a simple, vertical, Greek, gnostic eschatology, an immediate translation to glory. Troubles, trouble in the churches it may be, spark Paul's momentary exit strategy, his longing to "depart and be with Christ."

On the other hand, he considered: "To remain in the flesh is more necessary on your account" (Phil 1:24). I am for you, so I should be with you. It is better for you that I am here. We can add: to raise my voice, to lift my voice, to write my letters, to preach my Gospel, to have influence into the next generation.

Paul longs for exit. Paul lives for voice.

How much for exit? How much for voice? How much reforming exit? How much institutional loyalty? How much reformation? How much counter-reformation? How much pulpit? How much table? How much discontinuity? How much continuity? How much new world? How much old world?

On these spiritual balances hangs the cure of our souls. Needless to say, there is not an answer, no formulaic response, no "one size fits all," no ethical Procrustean bed. Another Pauline verse beckons: "Only let each one be fully convinced in his own mind" (Rom 14:5). We could, in faith, though, at least carry away some—four—shared understandings as people of faith.

We understand that, on a daily (if not hourly) basis, we are choosing, by the freedom of the will, between exit and voice. To have voice means to have to stay. To exit means to give up voice. To exit may be your statement, your voice, within a certain context, but then it is your valediction, your swan song. On the other hand, your voice may be your exit, but then it is a prophetic utterance, with all the continuing costs attested in the four greater and twelve lesser prophecies of our Hebrew scripture.

We understand that most decisions involve some admixture, some balance—neither only Webster nor only Calhoun; but the shadow of Henry Clay, the great compromiser, on the way to a common hope.

We understand that where we place our physical self, our body, our standard on the field of battle—our social location— makes a difference. Starting with showing up for worship, to speak with our neighbors, to sing the hymns of faith, to utter our prayers, and to attend to the Word.

We understand, too, that whatever voice we lift, even the muted voice of silent witness, has a hearing, makes a difference, marks our faith, and influences the faith of others.

Coda

Exit? Voice?

Both will mean *upomone*—longsuffering, longsuffering, longsuffering.

Press on, dear one, press on. Big steps are better than small steps. But small steps are better than no steps. And no steps are better than backward steps.

Take heart for the long journey, the daily exit from the green garden, and the hourly summons of the dominical voice. Take the spirit of Paul in Philippians with you. Take some radiance with you this morning. "God does not die on the day when we cease to believe in a personal Deity, but we die on the day when our lives cease to be illumined by the steady radiance, renewed daily, of a wonder, the source of which is beyond all reason."[4]

Exit or voice?

You be the judge.

In that strange American English idiom: *it's up to you.*

---

4. Hammarskjold, *Markings*, 88.

Sweet Chariot

2 Kings 2:1–12
Wednesday, August 9th, 2017

In (or near) the year 850 BC, the prophet Elijah stood against the prophets of Baal on Mt. Carmel. He alone stood against four hundred fifty. The enemy prophets called on Baal to bring fire. Baal did not, but Yahweh did, at Elijah's imprecation: "Cry aloud, for he is a god. Either he is musing. Or he is inside. Or he is on a journey. Or he is asleep—he needs to wake up. Maybe he does not hear well. Try again" (1 Kgs 18:27). Elijah also announced the end of a great drought. On the way to the river Jordan.

In the year 820 BC, Elijah went up a high mountain, not unlike that on which Jesus stood in Mark, and listened for God. He heard God. Not in fire, smoke, whirlwind, techno wizardry, or techno frenzy. For God was not there. But in a still small voice. In silence, the silence before hearing and speech. In conscience. In mind and will: "The Lord passed by, and a great strong wind rent the mountains and broke in pieces the rocks before the Lord, but the Lord was not in the wind; and after the wind an earthquake, but the Lord was not in the earthquake; and after the earthquake a fire, but the Lord was not in the fire; and after the fire—a still, small voice" (1 Kgs 19:11–12). On the way to the river Jordan.

In the year 800 BC, Elijah, the troubler of Israel, saw King Ahab, through his wife, Jezebel, take the garden of a poor man,

Naboth, and kill Naboth in the process.[1] *I will give you a better vineyard for it.* But Naboth did not want another, but his own. *And Ahab sulked, vexed and sullen, and lay down on his bed, and turned his face, and would eat no food.* But Naboth held onto his vineyard. *But Jezebel said, 'Do you govern Israel? Arise and eat bread and let your heart be cheerful. I will get you the vineyard of Naboth the Jezreelite.* But Naboth resisted her, too. *So they took him outside the city and stoned him to death. And Jezebel said, go and take Naboth's vineyard, for he is dead.* But Elijah confronted the king. *Have you killed and taken? Then I tell you—In the place where dogs licked up the blood of Naboth shall dogs lick your own blood.* Elijah, the troubler of Israel. It is one thing to desire another's property, and another to take it by force. Elijah held a mirror before the country that wanted such a king, and the influence of such a queen. The Bible has a long history of contention against cruel authority. On the way to the river Jordan.

In the year 30 AD, Elijah's spirit awakened Peter, who went up a high mountain with Jesus to see Him changed. Elijah brought reason and morality to the religion Moses founded. Summer is meant to remind us of the priority of worship. Find a way to get to worship. Worship brings the insight of personal need, lifted in prayer. Worship brings the insight of another's hurt, lifted in communal singing, four-part harmonic hymns. Worship brings the insight of clarity, a word fitly spoken, lifted in the sermon. Worship brings the insight of choosing, the choice of faith, not thrill but will, lifted in the invitations, to devotion, discipline, dedication. Worship brings the insight of loyalty, of heart, lifted every Sunday in the offering of gifts and tithes. Make a choice. Elijah brought hope, prophetic hope, into the tradition and minds of his people. On the way from the river Jordan.

In the year 1735 AD, the spirit of Elijah rested on the New England community of North Hampton and the ministry of a Puritan divine, Jonathan Edwards, our Calvinist interlocutor this Lent. Edwards saw the divine light shining in the human soul. Edwards saw that the material universe exists in God's mind. Edwards

1. For the following story and passages in context, see 1 Kings 21.

saw faith in the willingness of saints to be damned for the glory of God. Edwards saw religious affections, inclinations, dispositions, all gifts of God in faith, the love of God that kindles joy, hope, trust, peace and "a sense of the heart." Edwards saw the centrality of the experience of faith: a person may know that honey is sweet, but no one can know what sweet means until they taste the honey. Edwards saw that "God delights properly in the devotions, graces, and good works of his saints." Jonathan Elijah Edwards, our New England precursor, walked along the Connecticut River, on the way from the river Jordan.

In the year 1865, in our nation's capital, the spirit of Elijah touched the tongue of Abraham Lincoln. Months and days before Lincoln died, Lincoln cried out: "With malice toward none, with charity for all, with firmness in the right as God gives us to see the right, let us finish the work that we are in."[2] Real cost, real costs, occasion our very freedom to gather in community for worship this morning. The same spirit of 850 BC, that presence, that quickened consciousness, that affection, that devotion, and that inclination were present with Lincoln, and they are with us today. You have the brute fact of the brute creation. You, too, have the spirit.

In the year 1951, the spirit of Elijah rested in the mind of Ray Bradbury. He wrote a book, *Fahrenheit 451* (this is the temperature at which paper burns), an eschatological prophecy about the end of books, the end of reading, and the end of memory. The novel ends along a river. Montag finds himself with hoboes around a campfire, along the river bank. He is surprised to find that fire, the mode of book destruction he has resisted, can "give as well as take, warm and well as burn." He waits in the shadows. The men around the fire summon him out of the dark, and take him in. He learns that each one of them has committed some book to memory. One is living Plato's *Republic*. One is the work of Thomas Hardy. One has memorized several of the plays of Shakespeare. Byron, Machiavelli, Tom Paine, and the gospels, Matthew, Mark, Luke and John—all these are carried in the minds of hoboes, walking libraries, the remaining memory of the art of the race. "What

2. Lincoln, "Second Inaugural Address," 477.

have you to offer?" they ask Montag. "Parts of Ecclesiastes and of the Revelation to St. John," he replies.[3] In 2015, an age that has eschewed reading for scanning, books for blogs, memory for google, and knowing for earning, Elijah Bradbury's word resonates. On the way out from the river Jordan.

In the year 1959, down in the southern third of Alabama, the spirit of Elijah rested in the mind of Harper Lee. She wrote a book, a great book, a book great because it changed people's minds and hearts. Like Augustine's *Confessions*, like *Uncle Tom's Cabin*, like the *Diary of Anne Frank*, like Elie Wiesel's *Night*, like what Tom Hanks tried to do with *Philadelphia*. The prophet's magic mantel, which divides the river Jordan, pierces the heart. Lee's pastor, our friend, Thomas Lane Butts, spoke of her to me some years ago. All on the way from the river Jordan.

In the year 1965, in early March, the spirit of Elijah walked across the Edmund Pettis Bridge in Selma, Alabama. John Lewis was there, as he said: "Not angry, but full of righteous indignation."[4] Through the history, offices, and gifts of Boston University, we sat next to him over dinner three years ago. He wanted to be a preacher, growing up: "I would come home and preach to the chickens," he remembered. If nothing else, perhaps fifty years hence we could remember that real change is real hard but comes in real time when people really work at it, on the ground, in personal conversation, then in small groups, with gifted leadership. Down on the way from the River Jordan.

In the winter of the year 2015, Elijah, the spirit of Elijah brooded over the face of New England snow fields. The sore muscles of a shoveling people, the tired torsos of a commuting community, the undaunted willingness still to help a neighbor, the gritty determination to get through the blizzard, the awareness of needs for investment in the communal forms of transport, the gladness of children, and the extra time of adults, the same spirit visited. But also, the sore memory muscles wrestling with the horror and mayhem—needless and cruel—of Marathon 2013.

3. Bradbury, *Fahrenheit 451*, 141.
4. At dinner with the author and his wife, Boston University, 2015.

The blizzard of feeling and thought inevitably brought by a current courtroom trial to the surface. The rush of anger alongside the search for the better angels of one's nature. You may not daily recognize Elijah. But he is present. Morning in reading. Mealtime in prayer. Evening in quiet. Sunday in worship. (People have such odd reasons for avoiding worship.) On the way forward from the river Jordan. Elijah: elusive spirit, mysterious ghost, the divine present absence personified.

On March 8th of 2015, the spirit of prophet Elijah hovered in the nave of Marsh Chapel, Boston University. Over many decades, the chapel has given beauty, grace, preachment, music, and recollection to you and others. Some here have found God, and some here have been found by God. Marsh—a gift. And so you have responded. By listening on the radio—good. By joining us one Sunday—good. By giving to and through this ministry—good. By inviting someone to listen, too. By inviting someone to come with you—good. By dreaming of an even more permanent place, and even stronger witness, and an even more vibrant voice at Marsh. One of you may choose to endow the deanship of this chapel—good. Elijah awaits us. On the way from the river Jordan.

In the year—I apologize, I have mislaid the exact date—the prophet Elijah will be on my doorstep and knocking at your door. Perhaps at midnight. Maybe at noon day. Possibly at dawn or in the wee hours of the morning. The eschatological prophet, the prophet of the last things, the one invited by Peter to a booth with Jesus, Elijah, the prophet of God, will make a pastoral visit. In the last hour of my life and yours. There will be the river Jordan. There will be a mantel slapped on the water. There will be a parting of the ways. There will be a step forward. There will be a chariot, a sweet chariot, a swinging sweet chariot, a fiery, swinging, sweet chariot. There will be a presence. Could it be that the weeks of cascade, the days of Nevada, the snow and snow and snow of our 2015 New England winter of discontent should carry an evocation, a query, a reminder, a call, a premonition, a measuring, a warning, a promise? Most of what we spend our time (and our money) on doesn't matter at all. It is the spirit that giveth life.

Thomas Lane Butts once said:

> Near the end of Nelle Harper Lee's wonderful novel, *To Kill a Mockingbird*, there is a touching and unforgettable scene. Jean Louise (Scout), the young daughter of the courageous Atticus Finch, has persuaded her father to let her come to the courtroom to hear the verdict in the controversial case in which he is defending a black man. She chose to sit in the balcony with the black people. The inevitable "guilty" verdict is rendered. It is over. Atticus Finch gathers his papers, places them in his briefcase, and begins a sad and lonely walk down the center aisle to the back door. Scout hears someone call her name, "Miss Jean Louise?" She looks behind her and sees that all of the black people are standing up as her father walks down the aisle. Then, she heard the voice of the black minister, Reverend Sykes: "Miss Jean Louise, stand up, stand up, your father's passing." Can you hear that? It begs to be heard.[5]

Here is one way to live. Elijah's way. The spirit way. The way of confidence born of obedience. The way of the journey of faith, the obedience of faith. In this way, we live with the trust to see things through. To cross over. To cross the river. To trust our past. To trust our experience. To trust the spirit. To trust our Elisha's, our friends and successors. To trust that, in some way spiritually similar to Elijah at Jordan, a sweet chariot awaits.

A chariot of promise. A chariot of freedom. A chariot of hope. A chariot of deliverance. A chariot of salvation. A chariot of heaven. A chariot to carry us home.

5. Butts, "Sermon from Monroeville Alabama United Methodist Church."

Forgiven

Luke 7:36

Thursday, August 10th, 2017

Introduction

Please forgive the intrusive nature of this sermon, for I want to begin by taking a walk with you into the attic of your soul. Though we are becoming acquainted, becoming friends, it is not my right to initiate such a visit. Though we are pastors and parishioners, it is not our right to force such a trek back up through the mist of time. You would need to make an invitation yourself. Even to suggest the climb, without any initiative on your part, is rude of me. I apologize.

The Gospel, however, intrudes upon our very souls, whether the preacher has a right or not. As kingfishers catch fire and dragonflies draw flame, so truth—that light in which we see light—advances upon us. So we go ahead. We walk together upstairs to the landing. You kindly have turned on the hall light. Thank you. I wonder if this is a sign from you that you will welcome this joint venture? We pull down in the chain that loosens the attic portal. You know how that little door in the ceiling falls open slowly and a flank of wooden stairs comes down, and down, and down, and touches our feet. We are ready to climb up into the darkness.

Watch your step. You have not been up into the cobwebs and the dust of memory, the mothballs and the coverlets of history, the grime and the darkness of the past. It is a little slow going. This is your attic, though. You know it as well as you know your own past. In fact, it is your past, box by box and crate by crate. I have no right to be here, and if you ask me, I will leave. A man has a right to his own regrets. They are not common property. They are yours, these boxes and labels and shoes and hangers and records and amulets and souvenirs from the dusty past. One of you is looking over at an old service uniform from the great war—brown and rumpled. Another sees bobby sox and a political poster—*I LIKE IKE*. She has stumbled past three old Beatles albums: greatest hits, *Abbey Road*, the White album. I notice a Jim Croce tape. I wonder if it still plays? He thumbs through a pile of other, newer albums. Of course there are lots of photographs. What kind of an attic would it be without boxes, records, and photographs? And who are those people in those pictures anyway?

This is the attic of memory. No, we won't stop at the wardrobe today. The wardrobe is for another day, a day of hope and imagination. Lions and witches come from wardrobes. Today we are looking back, though. We are going to stumble and claw our way over into the back corner. There is not much light here. It is a long time since anyone came back in, all this way. Dust, cobwebs—it makes you sneeze.

Over in the corner, there is a small, low box, carefully closed and tied around with a little bailer's twine. This is yours. No one else knows it is here or, if they do, they have forgotten, never understood it, or just don't care. But you know and remember and understand and care. I really do not want to be here, and you probably don't want to either. I—for it is not my business. You—because, in black ink, now dusty, a single, awful, hellish word is penned across the top of the box: regret. Regret is a short synonym for hell. And up here, in the attic of memory, off in the corner, sits this stupid box, which means nothing to anyone except you. There it is—a single box labeled "regret."

Open it.

Go ahead. Try it. If you want. I think you have wanted to come up here but just never had 20 minutes of quiet to do so. Remember last summer when you thought about the box? And remember that early morning dream? That was a strange thing. I want to encourage you to open it. Hold it in both hands. Untie the twine. Loosen the top. Turn it over and let it all fall out.

That was a gutsy thing to do. Good for you.

The reason the box was marked "regret" is that this is one thing you regret. You have a regret. That is part of being human. Can you live with being human? Can you live with being a little lower than the angels? How do I know all this? As my great aunt would say, "If you're so smart, how come you aren't rich?" A real good question. I know because I have boxes in my attic too. They, too, are covered with cobwebs. I, too, make my visits, my attic climbs, very seldom. And yes, I know about regret. Not just vicariously, either. There is nothing quite as bitter. If only . . .

I asked to come up here with you for a reason. Up in the attic, here, with that swinging, bare lightbulb, the Johnny Mathis record, and all this dust, we may feel God.

Look at the box again and all its contents spread across the floor. In the dark, I cannot see the floor, but after forty years and ten pulpits, I truly doubt if any of it would surprise me. After reading the Bible and Shakespeare and a few decades worth of the New York Times, there is not much that surprises. But it is different for you. This is your attic, your memory, your box, your regret. It is *yours*. In a way, this box is more yours than any of the others.

In this box are the articles of impeachment brought by life against us. They are multiple and they are damning and unlike civil and criminal law, the laws of the soul do not give way to lawyerly cunning. And there is no vote, no two-thirds majority needed.

What is that you say? Not you? Never a cutting word? Never a selfish deed? Never an unhealthy habit? Never a compulsive trend? Never a myopic judgment? Never a temptation accepted? Never an ungenerous year? Never a non-giving decade? Not you? Never a misspent dollar or day or dream? You don't go to enough funerals.

But the box doesn't lie. Nor does the conscience. Nor does the memory. Nor does life.

It simply spells "regret." That, I regret.

God Forgives You

There is something that both can and must be said as we pack up the regret box. It is not a human thing to say, though we are the only saying beings around so we do the best we can. It is a God word. And only God speaks God words.

First, looking down at the dusty cardboard of past regret— something that can fester and infect and cripple if not removed— first there is this. God forgives you. It is, according to the Scripture, the divine promise and intention to forgive and to forgive. Abraham felt it. Joseph practiced it. Hosea proclaimed it. Jesus taught us to pray for it. And for two-thousand years, the church has tried to exemplify, embody this one word. God forgives. John Wesley asked his preachers one initial question: "Do you know God to be a pardoning God?" Now that, in the face of a box marked "regret," that is good news. In the face of the worst rejection and the most regrettable misjudgment on earth, God practices a powerful forgiveness.

You know, in the midst of all the harshness of the religious right and the flightiness of the secular left, it can be hard to hear the central truth about God and about us. God forgives.

God forgives before we are up in the attic at all. God forgives when we realize what we have to regret. God forgives as we carry the regret around. God forgives when we hear and when we do not and it does not depend on our hearing.

Do you know God to be a pardoning God? If so, you know God, the God of Jesus Christ.

Here are Scriptures worth memorizing about God who forgives:

> If you forgive others their trespasses, your Heavenly Father will also forgive you. (Matt 6:14)
>
> Lord how often shall my brother sin against me and I forgive him? As many as seven times? . . . I do not say to you seven times, but seventy times seven. (Matt 18:21)
>
> Be kind to one another, tenderhearted, forgiving one another as God in Christ has forgiven you. (Eph 4:32)

Other People Forgive You

But maybe that is not what keeps you awake, not what makes you linger today in the attic. You may well believe and trust that God forgives, but what about those you have regrettably hurt?

This can be particularly hard for those who have grown up around especially hardened parents and other adults. If you have not heard an encouraging word much growing up, it can be hard to believe that, later in life, those other humans around you can be gracious. They can be.

As a matter of fact, most of the time they are. More than most of the time. People forgive, more than you know and more than you may think you deserve. It really delights me. People have a profound capacity to forgive and forget. It is God given, and it is real and it is good.

- I think of the waiting father and the prodigal son.
- I think of Paul forgiving Peter's two faced behavior.
- I think of Augustine's mother forgiving his selfishness.
- I think of Erasmus forgiving the wayward Popes.
- I think of Grant and Lee at Appomatox.
- I think of Abraham Lincoln walking through Richmond.
- I think of the Marshall Plan and rebuilding of Germany in the 1940s.
- I think of women and men, night after day, for millenia.

You may have to ask sometime for forgiveness. You probably should. Say, "I'm sorry." Like the Fonz, who could never utter the words, "I was wrong." But my experience is that most people, most of the time, when confronted with a heartfelt, sincere apology from a person of integrity will say, "Don't worry about it. I forgive you." It is one of the greatest things about other people. You may have to give it a little time. You may have to pray about it. You may have to trust a little. But—other people will forgive you.

Forgiving Yourself

But that may not be what holds you here in the attic. As a matter of fact, I bet that the box is still up here, wrapped in twine and covered with dirt and marked regret for another reason. It's one thing for God to forgive you. It's one thing to accept another's kindness. But in the end, that still leaves you a few sandwiches short of a picnic and a few french fries short of a happy meal. God has forgiven you! Your neighbor has forgiven you! Now comes the hard part.

You have to forgive yourself. You have to let yourself off the hook. You have to find a way to admit to yourself that you are not 101 percent perfect. You have to, well, accept your own acceptance. Didn't Paul Tillich once say something like that? And that can be a lot easier said than done. Because we have a way of holding onto what poisons us. We have a way of just wrapping ourselves in a miserable kind of self-conceited self-condemnation. Up in the attic.

Sunday is a good time to dump your guilt. God doesn't want it. No neighbor finally has much use for it. So why is it still in the box? What good is it? Get rid of it. When in doubt, throw it out.

God forgives you. So does your neighbor. Forgive yourself.

Matter of fact, while we are here, up in the attic—let's just take that box out of here. I'll hold the ladder for you while you're coming down. You can carry it with a little homiletical help. If we hurry, we can get it out on the curb before noon, and the heavenly garbage truck always comes by this part of your mental world Sunday at noon. There, it's out on the curb, and soon it will be gone for good. William Blake:

> And throughout all eternity
> I forgive you, you forgive me.
>
> And throughout all eternity
> I forgive you, you forgive me.
>
> And throughout all eternity
> I forgive you, you forgive me.[1]

---

1. Blake, "Broken Love," 57.

Theological Temptations

John 8:32

Friday, August 11th, 2017

Preface

Your love of Christ shapes your love of Scripture and tradition and reason and experience. You are lovers and knowers too. We are ever in peril of loving what we should use and using what we should love, to paraphrase Augustine. In particular, we sometimes come perilously close to the kind of idolatry that uses what we love. We are tempted, for our love Christ, to force a kind of certainty upon what we love, to use what is meant to give confidence as a force and form of certainty. It is tempting to substitute the security and protection of certainty for the freedom and grace of confidence. But faith is about confidence not certainty. If we had certainty, we would not need faith.

1. Errancy

Your love for Christ shapes your love of Scripture. You love the Bible. You love its psalmic depths. Psalm 130 comes to mind. You love its stories and their strange names. Obededom comes to mind. You love proverbial wisdom. One sharpens another comes to mind. You love its freedom, its account of the career of freedom. The exodus comes to mind. You love its memory of Jesus. His holding children comes to mind. You love its honesty about religious life. Galatians comes to mind. You love its strangeness. John comes to mind. You love the Bible like Rudolph Bultmann loved it, enough to know it through and through.

You rely on the Holy Scripture to learn to speak of faith and as a medium of truth for the practice of faith. Today, around our amphitheater, in worship, we share this reliance and this love. The fascinating multiplicity of hearings, here, and the interplay of congregations—present, absent, near, far, known, unknown, religious, and unreligious—have a common ground in regard for the Scripture. Graduates of Ohio Wesleyan University, Presbyterians from Pittsburgh, Methodists from Rochester, and a preacher from Boston all share today in the hearing. One listens to this service to hear the interpretation of the gospel. Another listens for the musical offerings and for the reading of Scripture. A student listens out of a love of Christ that embraces a love of Scripture. Here, scholars, teachers, and students have in common, by their love for Christ, a love for the Scripture, too. In this way, may we all affirm Mr. Wesley's motto: *homo unius libri*, to be a person of one book.

But the Bible is errant. It is theologically tempting for us to go on preaching as if the last 250 years of study just did not happen. They did. That does not mean that we should deconstruct the Bible to avoid allowing the Bible to deconstruct us, or that we should study the Bible in order to avoid allowing the Bible to study us. In fact, after demythologizing the Bible, we may need to re-mythologize the Bible too. It is the confidence born of obedience, not some certainty born of fear that will open the Bible to us. We need not fear truth, however it may be known. So Luke may not have had all his geographical details straight. John 8 includes the woman caught in adultery—but not in its earliest manuscripts. Actually she, poor woman, is found, in some texts, at the end of Luke. Paul did not write the document from the earlier third century, 3 Corinthians. The references to slavery in the New Testament are as errant and time-bound as are the references to women not speaking in church. The references to women not speaking in church are as errant and time bound as are the references to homosexuality. The references to homosexuality are as errant and time bound as are the multiple lists of the twelve disciples. The various twelve listings are as errant and time bound as the variations between John and the other Gospels.

Now my pulpit, the Marsh Chapel pulpit, and others like it, are not within traditions which affirm the Scripture as the sole source of religious authority. We do not live within a Sola Scriptura tradition. The Bible is primary, foundational, fundamental, basic, prototypical—but not exclusively authoritative. Do you hear that? It begs to be heard. Today's passage from John is within an idealized memory of something that may or may not have happened in the way accounted, somewhere long ago in Galilee. It looks back sixty years. What do you remember from January of 1957? Nor was it written for that kind of certainty. It is formed in the faith of the church to form the faith of the church.

If I were teaching a Sunday School class in Nebraska this winter, I would buy the class copies of Throckmorton's Gospel parallels and read it with them.

We grasp for certainty, but confidence grasps us.

2. *Equality*

You love the tradition of the church as well. Though with a scornful wonder we see her sore oppressed. Participants at Chautauqua love the church's tradition too, enough to study it, to know it, and to seek its truth. The central ecclesiastical tradition of his time, the tradition of apostolic succession, John Wesley termed a "fable." It would be like political debaters today using charged language like "fairy tale." Likewise, we lovers of the church tradition will not be able to grasp certainty in it if that grasping dehumanizes others. The Sabbath was made for the human being, not the other way around, in our tradition.

Baptism is as traditional and central a variously understood practice as Christianity possesses. It is, in some ways, the very doorway to our traditions. Yet listen to Paul today. In his context, he rejects baptism. For him gospel trumps tradition.

Our linkage of the gifts of heterosexuality and ministry, however traditional, fall before grace and freedom. Further, on a purely practical level, another generation will not be impressed by church growth strategies rooted in the exclusion of 10 percent of the population. There is a serious upside limit to the use of gay bashing to grow churches. My three children in their twenties are not going to stay around for it.

It is theologically tempting to shore up by keeping out, but it has no future. Equality will triumph over exclusion. You cannot exclude your way to life. *It is coming like the glory of the morning on the wave.*[1]

If I were convening a Lenten study in suburban Washington DC, I would have the group read Gary Wills's *Head and Heart: American Christianities*, for some perspective on the way traditions change. Read Edward Bishop, *Half Has Never Been Told: Slavery and the Making of American Capitalism.*[2]

3. *Evolution*

You love the mind, the reason. You love the prospect of learning. You love the life of the mind. You love the Lord with heart, soul, and mind. A mind is a terrible thing to waste. You love the reason in the same way that Charles Darwin, a good Anglican, loved the reason. You love its capacity to see things differently.[3] But you know what? 35 percent of Americans disbelieve in evolution!

Of course reason unfettered can produce hatred and holocaust. Learning for its own sake needs virtue and piety. More than anything else, learning to last must finally be rooted in loving. Did you hear the one thing requested in our vibrant Psalm? To inquire in the temple. Inquiry!

1. Howe, "Battle Hymn of the Republic," 717.

2. See Wills, *Head and Heart*, and Bishop, *Half Has Never Been Told*.

3. During the summer of 2009, Marsh Chapel hosted a series of ten sermons on the theme, "Darwin and Faith," offered by preachers from around the country.

The universe is 14 billion years old. The earth is 4.5 billion years old. 500 million years ago, multi-celled organisms appeared in the Cambrian explosion. 400 million years ago, plants sprouted. 370 million years ago, land animals emerged. 230 million years ago, dinosaurs appeared (and disappeared 65 million years ago). 200,000 years ago, hominids arose. Every human being carries 60 new mutations out of 6 billion cells. Yes, evolution through natural selection by random mutation is a reasonable hypothesis, says Francis Collins, father of the human genome project—and, strikingly, a person of faith.

If I were the chaplain of a small private school in New England, I might have my fellowship group read Collins's *Language of God* this winter.[4] He can teach us to reason together.

It is tempting to disjoin learning and vital piety, but it is not loving to disjoin learning and vital piety. They go together. The God of Creation is the very God of Redemption. Their disjunction may help us cling for a while to a kind of faux certainty. But their conjunction is the confidence born of obedience. Falsehood has no defense and truth needs none.

4. *Existence*

You love experience. The gift of experience in faith is the heart of your love of Christ. You love Christ. Like Howard Thurman loved the mystical ranges of experience, you do too. Isaiah, in looking forward, can sing of the joy of harvest. We know joy. Joy seizes us. Joy grasps us when we are busy grasping at other things. You love what we are given morning and evening.

You love experience more than enough to examine your experience, to think about and think through what you have seen and done.

But beloved, a simple or general appeal to the love of experience, in our time, in 2017, in this coming decade of humiliation, is not appealing or loving. It is not experience but our very existence

---

4. See Collins, *Language of God.*

which lies under the shadow of global violence. To have any future worthy of the name, we shall need to foreswear preemptive violence. How the stealthy entry of such a manner of behavior could enter our civil discourse without voluminous debate and vehement challenge is a measure of our longing for false certainties. In discussions (or lack of discussions) about violent action that is preemptive, unilateral, imperial, and reckless, our existence itself is on the line. One thinks of Lincoln saying of slavery: "Those who support it might want to try it for themselves."[5] Not one of us wants to be the victim of preemptive violence. We may argue about the need for response and even for the need of some kinds of anticipatory defense. But preemption? It will occlude existence itself.

If I were gathering a book club in downtown Boston to read this winter, I would select the articles and books of Andrew Bacevich. Our future lies on the narrower path of responsive, communal, sacrificial, prudent behavior and requires of us, in Bacevich's hero Neibuhr's phrase, "a spiritual discipline against resentment."[6]

There are, indeed, theological temptations in the unbalanced love of Scripture, tradition, reason, or experience. As we come soon to Lent, let us face them down. Let us face them down together. Let us do so by lifting our voices to admit errancy, affirm equality, explore evolution, and admire existence. The measure of preaching today in the tradition of a responsible Christian liberalism is found in our willingness to address errancy, equality, evolution, and existence.

Coda

Perhaps we could set to music a hymn with these verses, in some combination:

> *God is love.*
> *Love is both mercy and justice, both compassion and holiness.*
> *Compassion is more important than holiness.*

5. Lincoln, "Address to an Indiana Regiment," 477.
6. Niebuhr quoted in Lasch, *True and Only Heaven*, 365.

God loves the world (not just the church).

The church lives in the culture. The church lives in the culture to transform it. (Not above it to disdain it, not below it to obey it, not behind it to mimic it, not before it hector it).

The church is the Body of Christ.

Christ is alive. Wherever there is way, truth, life . . .

Life is sacred.

Life is a sacred journey to freedom.

The Bible is freedom's book.

The Bible is a source—not the source—of truth

The Sabbath was made for man, not man for the Sabbath.

War is hell.

Peace is heaven. Jesus is the prince of Peace.

Gay people are people.

Women's bodies are women's bodies.

Women and men need each other.

There is a self-correcting spirit of truth loose in the universe.

The founder of Methodism is John Wesley (not John Calvin).

The ministers of the conference are the conference. Period.

Ministry is preaching.

The fun of faith is in tithing and inviting. 'Remember the poor.'

Tithing is required. It is core, not elective.

Death is the last enemy. As Forest Gump said, atop his beloved's grave, "My momma told me that 'death is a part of life,' but I wish it weren't."

God's love outlasts death.

A Tradition of Principled Resistance

Luke 4:1–13

Sunday, February 25th, 2007

Marsh Chapel at Boston University

It is the season of Lent and, again, come this first Sunday in Lent, we meet Jesus in the wilderness. There He resists. In the time honored tradition of a three part story, we are given a lesson about making and keeping human life—human. Here, as in our other gospels, the Lord faces and masters the various temptations which we also know. They include a kind of will to power, a sort of pride, and a type of avarice. We come to church with some experience of temptation and resistance. As the song writer says, "good experience comes from seasoned judgment—which comes from bad experience."

In many communities, including our own, the sun rises this morning—this Lenten morning—on experience of loss and hurt. This morning, there are homes and families who have suddenly known unexpected loss. This morning, there are friends and groups of friends who have been faced with mortal danger. At one breakfast table, a wife now sits alone on a Sunday for the first time in sixty years. At another breakfast table, a family gathers for the first time, in a long time, and is missing a member. It would help us to remember just how short our words fall in trying to describe the depth of these moments. Our words arrive only at the shoreline, at the margin of things. Beyond this, we practice prayer, a kind of sitting silent before God.

Today, our immediate community, here, along the Charles River, mourns unexpected losses in a recent, tragic fire. Along with the scripture and the music, amid the hymns and prayers of our worship, there also walks among us today, by the mind's farther roads, a recognition of loss. There is some shock to loss. There is a kind of fear that comes with loss. There is, often later, an honest anger. There is some numbness. There is a real—and good—desire to do something helpful. There are questions, numerous and important. And there is the one haunting question, too, why?

We do not know why these things happen. We hurt and grieve. In the bones. At the deeper levels, we just do not know, and for a community committed to knowing more and more, this means wandering in a serious wilderness. Give us an equation to solve. Show us a biography that needs writing. Provide us with an experiment. Happily, we would organize a committee, develop a proposal, or phone a list of donors. But loss, unexpected and unfair, is tragic. The tragic sense of life takes us out into wilderness, where we learn to resist.

Faith is resistance. Faith is the power to withstand what we cannot understand.

This morning, we are in worship to attest to something. Faith is the power to withstand what we cannot understand. Worship is the practice of faith by which we learn to withstand what we cannot understand. God is the presence, force, truth, and love Who alone deserves worship, and worship is the practice of the faith by which we learn to withstand what we cannot understand. Worship prepares us to resist. So we see Jesus again in the wilderness. To resist all that makes human life inhuman. So here you are, come lent, come Sunday, come this Sunday.

This week you may, suddenly, find that a choice is required of you, through no fault, intention, planning, or device of your own. Further, the choice you want to make perhaps could involve refusal and resistance: refusal of a request from an archetypal authority, resistance to a popular mood, resistance to an ingrained habit, refusal of the pleas of a friend. Russell Lowell predicts that, at least once, such a moment comes to every person and group to decide.

With all your heart you may want to refuse, to refuse. An invitation, a suggestion, a promotion, a direction, an order. *Your heart may say: this is not me, not right, not good.* Resistance always costs. Resistance means sacrifice. Resistance hurts. The slings and arrow of fortune's discontent draw blood. Resistance, refusal. Does such principled denial have a place in Christian living? Dare ask: Does God evoke and use refusal? Does Christ, God's everlasting Yes—in whom Paul says there is no longer yea and nay, but only Yes—does Christ desire resistance and refusal?

For Daniel, refusal to give up his family name and his religion, his faith landed him, with the others, in trouble. You enjoy the story, I know. Daniel resists the order to blaspheme and accepts punishment, even death. Bound in the heart of fire, the prophet of God is protected, strangely, by God who answers prayer.

For Naboth, refusal came more dear. Old King Ahab had every vineyard he wanted but one. He asked for the land. Naboth refused. He asked again, this time presumably in a more kingly voice. Naboth refused. Ahab asked again, with a hint of threat on his tongue. Naboth refused. And Ahab went whimpering to bed. Not so, Jezebel, who simply took Naboth aside and cut off his head. Refusal can either cost you a king's friendship, your head, or both.

John of Patmos did something to put himself out on the rocky prison isle, a first-century Papillon, as he wrote his Revelation, our last Bible book. Refusing to worship Caesar? Names jeeringly attached to Rome—beast, satan, whore? Resistance to the more established synagogue?

What if I were to shout to you this morning that this church had received a magnificent bequest, a precious gift, left to us by an ancestor? Further, were I to announce that this one gift was worth more than all of our buildings, all of our current endowment, and all of our church program put together? Would you not dance, sing, and soar?

You inherit a tradition of principled refusal, a pearl of great price, a treasure hidden in a field, a precious gift. A tradition of principled refusal.

Several summers ago, an older woman was robbed at gunpoint in her own home. The newspaper, perhaps accurately, has quoted her in full as regards her view of this crime: "We are raising a generation of hooligans."

Pummeled still, even in old age, even in closeted retirement, the violent spirit of the age pounds at her, lacing her with blows left and right. Yet she resists! You may recognize her, now.

This was Rosa Parks. A younger Mrs. Parks found herself seated midway back in a Montgomery bus, on December 1st, 1955, pummeled again by the hand of aggression, the Strong Man of this world. For some reason, she refused to move. Bus stopped. Police came. Crowd gathered. Anger, shouting. The Montgomery bus boycott began. A tradition of principled resistance—this is your native land, your mother tongue, your home territory.

The prophets of old knew this. They spoke about God's unbending holiness. They spoke about God's own refusal to set a divine seal on any present moment, any present setup, any present arrangement of power. They spoke about human suffering, about how God sees, hears, knows, remembers, and intervenes for the suffering. They spoke about God's justice, critical of every established power. They refused. Here it is: "Prophetic speech . . . [is] an act of relentless hope that refuses to despair, that refuses to believe that the world is closed off in patterns of exploitation and oppression."[1]

My son had only one request for a gift one year. He showed me a catalogue that pictured a little grill, for cooking meat, "a lean, mean, fat-reducing machine, guaranteed to reduce each average hamburger by 3 oz of fat—$59.95" Then I noticed the sponsor of this culinary instrument: George Foreman. And I inflicted a story on my son, as parents do.

In 1974, one of the greatest boxing matches of the century pitted Muhammad Ali against the world champion, George

1. Brueggeman, *Like Fire in the Bones*, 81.

Foreman. Kinshasha, Zaire. November 2nd. Ali predicted: "The most spectacular wonder human eyes have ever witnessed." Sixty thousand cheering fans, shouting, "Ali Bu Mal Ye," which antiseptically translated means, "Go get him."

Scenes: Foreman charging, rounds one to six. Foreman, 25, young, strong, powerful. Recently defeated both Frazier and Norton. Ali, 32, guile fitness and will. After five rounds, Foreman arm weary and bewildered. Third round, Ali leans to crowd: "He don't hurt me much." Fifth round, Foreman tantalized by the stationary target, angry, frustrated. Angelo Dundee had loosened the ropes! Ali, later: "The bull is stronger but the matador is smarter." Then, eighth round: "Ali is leaning back against the ropes, inviting the champion's hardest blows, when suddenly, in the next instant, he springs forward and brought Foreman down. Down the strong man went, the first time ever he had been knocked out."

In this country, the historic Christian church has been on the ropes for a generation, 30 years of blows to the midsection. God's spirit is not in a mode of lightening triumph, for those who would still maintain a real connection between deep personal faith and active social involvement. But the eighth round is still coming.

Those who may need to resist and refuse today are part of the spiritual rope strategy, the wearying of the Strong Man, the resistance of evil, the binding of evil. It's not pleasant. Hurt, setbacks, delay, confusion. But there is an eighth round coming! There is an eighth round coming!

How hungry the church is to perceive this truth today. God is at work, in part, to encourage and give stamina to those on the ropes, using Ali's rope-a-dope strategy, binding the Strong Man.

A tradition of principled resistance.

I can imagine an objection or two. Well taken, is your perhaps silent objection thus far: some refusal is Godly, but some is not. Too often those who resist or refuse are simply petulant, immature, arrogant, slothful, idiotic, and selfish. Agreed—but we speak here not of forms of hypocrisy, so many they are. Rather, we speak of principled resistance, which shows its character by enduring body blows, by leaning against the rope and aching.

Or maybe you doubt that refusal takes a part of small stage play. Perhaps only the civil disobedience of Gandhi, the peaceful resistance of Martin Luther King, or the risky French Resistance of Albert Camus stand out, great historic refusals, great moments of common endurance. But you would be wrong, I suggest, to think so. Most resistance is hidden, unheralded, unknown, and unrewarded. Most principled refusal is known only to the one sagging against the ropes, the one catching the body blows. Most real principled resistance is very ordinary.

Tithing is primarily a form of spiritual refusal, refusal to accept the world's understanding of success and refusal to accept the implication that all that we have is ours alone. Worship is primarily a form of spiritual refusal, refusal to accept the world's time clock, where all time is meant for work or play. Marriage and loyal friendship are primarily forms of spiritual refusal, refusal to accept the world's low estimate of intimacy, refusal to accept the unholy as good. Choosing carefully is primarily a form of spiritual resistance: "We live in a society that primarily starves our soul . . . we have to really resist the culture to care for the soul . . . [but] if we choose with care our professions and ways we spend our time and our homes in which we live, if we take care of our families and don't see them as problems, and if we nurture our relationships and friendships and marriages, then the soul probably will not show its complaints so badly."[2]

You are a part of a tradition of principled resistance.

In 350 BC, Philip of Macedon wanted to unite Greece, which he did—except for Sparta. He did everything he could. Finally, he sent them a note: if you do not submit at once I will invade your country. If I invade, I will pillage and burn everything in sight. If I march into Laconia, I will level your great city to the ground. The Spartans sent back this one-word reply: "If." (Laconic.)

You may not need this word today. You may want to remember it, though, especially if you are young. For one day, one day, you may want to use some of your spiritual bequest, your prophetic

2. Moore, *Care of the Soul*, 217.

endowment. You may need to draw on the tradition of principled refusal.

Good news has it that, along the ropes and upon the cross, Jesus has bound up the Strong Evil, subverting by being subject to it, and so empowered us to resist. A year before he was executed by the Nazis, languishing in a small prison cell, Dietrich Bonhoeffer wrote this hymn:

> By gracious powers so wonderfully sheltered
> and confidently waiting, come what may,
> We know that God is with us night and morning
> And never fails to greet us each new day.[3]

3. Bonhoeffer, *By Gracious Powers*, 517.

A Little Summer Beauty

Matthew 13:31–52
Monday, July 30th, 2017
Marsh Chapel at Boston University

Ant

The beauty of summer, *sub specie aeternitatis,* and particularly in a climate like yours, long in darkness and deep in cold, the beauty that is of the four score summers God gives you, at the largest extent of God's favor, is itself a matter for parabolic teaching in the spirit of the Gospel for the day. Let us meditate together for a few minutes today by taking a homiletical walk, down a dusty summer road, watching for a little beauty. In the mind's eye and with the sun upon our backs, let us meander a moment and see what we can see. After all, Jesus taught in parables, "teaching not one thing without a parable" (Mark 4:34).

Start small. There, in front of your left moccasin moves a lonely red ant, the lowliest of creatures, yet, like a Connecticut Yankee, bursting with the two revolutionary virtues, industry and frugality. Benjamin Franklin, admiring such frugality and industry (and dubious of much dogmatic preaching), wrote, "None preaches better than the ant, and he says nothing."[1] A good reminder.

While we step around the ant, the little insect recalls others: grasshoppers, flies, locusts. Simple creatures. Some of our friends prefer the heat of the West, and its insects, to the rain of the East,

1. Franklin, "Poor Richard's Almanac, 1735," 319.

8

and ours. The locusts, burning dry heat, flat arid landscape, and lack of water, out West, would seem to offer no competition. Yet, some love the virtue of the good people known there. Some like the simple rhythm of town life and enjoy the simple summer gatherings—reunions, little league, band concerts, parades. "The people there—they are folks with good hearts." And as Jesus taught his students, "If people have some measure of goodness themselves, think how good their maker must be."

Maybe that is the beauty of summer, to pause and appreciate simple, good people, folks with good hearts.

Berry

We can stop up the path just a bit. Raspberries, blackberries, all kinds of wild fruit are plentiful now. Jesus taught us to ask, simply, for bread and a name. We need food and forgiveness daily. Give us each day our daily bread and forgive us our sins, for we forgive all who are indebted to us. What bread does for the body, pardon does for the soul. One of the gifts of summer is the time and leisure to remember this. For this reason, a church should be fullest in the summer, this recognition of our ultimate needs.

Our neighbor has baked some of these wild berries into morning muffins. We stop to savor them with butter and coffee. We listen to one another along the path. So we are nourished by one another and made ready for the next steps in the journey.

Maybe this is the beauty of summer—to pause and make space for real worship, for that which can feed our hungers, and set us free for the next adventure.

Fence

Up ahead there is an old fence. For a river to be a river, it needs riverbanks high enough to contain the flowing water. For a lake to hold its integrity, it needs a shoreline that stands and lasts. For a field to retain any semblance of usefulness, it needs fences to mark its beginnings and endings. For an individual to have any identity, one needs the limits of positive improvement, as Jesus taught about perseverance, and of protective caution, as Jesus taught about times of trial. For a life to have meaning and coherence, it needs those riverbanks, shorelines, fences, and limits that give life shape and substance.

We can spend some summertime mending fences. Especially at a time and across a country so keenly divided, a house divided against itself. It is hard work, but utterly crucial. Keep your friendships in good repair and mend the fences where they need it. Think, heal, write, love.

Some years ago, I came by this same old fence. I was walking with my dad, as it happened. We had some coffee and a muffin. Then we started off together, down the old road, he to walk with a gnarled walking stick, and I to jog after my own eccentric fashion. But for a mile up to the same fence, to the place where the road parts, we walked together. We shuffled and talked a little, remembering the name of a former neighbor, spotting a new garden planted, making a plan or two for later on. We remembered an old friend, a old-style doctor, long dead. He remembered that Dr. Thro came to visit him the day his mother died. "It's hard when your mother dies," he said, "It gets you right in the chest!" I remembered Dr. Thro swimming the length of the lake and, while he did so, barking various orders at the universe and some of this patients along the shoreline, riverbank, fence—along the virtuous limits that make a life. We came to fork, one taking the high road and one the low, and, with that—an embrace and a word and a glance—we were alone again. Now, along that fence, summer by summer, I walk with my dad again, feeling him beside me.

Maybe this is the beauty of summer, to set limits and keep them, to mend our fences and protect them, to honor one another in faith and love.

Cloud

This is a clear day, in our reverie, but even so, there are a few dancing clouds, white and bright. We try to make sense of the summer and to make space for the summer; to honor this season, one that brings together meteorological splendor and theological insight. In our chapel, we put together different summer experiences—a wedding and luncheon one day, a talk on Summer reading another, a brunch to honor parents, dads, and all, a singing Vacation Bible School for the Young and Young at Heart, a Holiday Brunch, an annual summer national preacher series, and fellowship each week on the plaza—to allow meteorology and theology to dance well together.

There is a dimension of possibility alive in the summer that is hard to approximate in the rest of the year. We alter our summer habits, not at all to suggest that devotion is less central now (for, in some ways, summer ought to be the most spiritual of the seasons) but rather to accommodate our life to the necessary rhythms of life around us.

It is astounding to hear again in the Gospel that the kingdom of heaven is hidden, small, lovely, precious, immaterial, consequential, and secret. But so Jesus teaches us, parable by parable. Summer is the season and devotion is the focus of all such wonder and possibility. Maybe this is the beauty of summer, to pause and allow a fuller consideration of all the possibilities around us.

Breeze

A summer wind accompanies us as we walk farther down the dirt road. A fawn—or was it a fox?—darts into the brush. The smell of apples, already ripening, greets us at the turn. More sun, bigger, higher, and hotter, makes us sweat.

I guess every family has a family secret or two, that one subject that dominates every present moment by the sheer weight of its hidden silence, that one taboo topic that somehow screams through its apparent muteness. Daddy's drinking. Junior's juvenile record. Grampa's prison term. The so-called elephant in the room. True of nations, too—and businesses, projects, and even churches. You find it, finally, by asking gently about what is feared.

The human family has this same kind of family secret. Something we avoid discussing, if at all possible, something that makes us fearful, something that dominates us through our code of silence. It is our mortality. Our coming death is the one thing that most makes us who we are, mortal, mortals, creatures, sheep in another's pasture, not perfect because not perfectible, the image of God but not God, "fear in a handful of dust." Yet we are so busy with so many other things that we avoid this elemental feature of existence.

In the face of death, we turn heavily upon our faith. It is the steady and warming wind, the breeze of the Holy Spirit, that keeps us and strengthens us all along the road. Here is the argument. If your children ask you for something, do you not provide it? And you are evil! (Not to put too fine a point on it!) Imagine, then, *how much more* God will provide for the children beloved of the all powerful, holy God. You are loved, beloved, graced, embraced—a child of the living God.

Maybe this is the beauty of summer, to number our days that we get hearts of wisdom, to measure the mystery about us and give over our imaginations to a consideration of our limits.

Neighbor

Walking along, you may conjure or contract a traveling bug. Shall we drive north? A popular refrain in Montreal runs like this: "Canada could have had the best of three worlds: British government, American industry, and French culture; instead, Canada collected the worst of all three: French bureaucracy, British economics, and American culture!"

But don't you believe it. As that proverb's tangled contents and tone of wry self-criticism tell, Canada has a great deal to offer you and me. We can learn from our northern neighbors. This is part testimony and part admonition: Take a look at the Dominion of Canada. In particular, let me suggest three things that we can bring across the border.

First, there is the Anglican Church of Canada. Its influence far exceeds that of its sister Protestant Episcopal church in the United States. Though still statistically small, Canadian Anglicanism is, in one sense, the ecclesiastical leader of its land. We United Methodists—especially those out of the Methodist Episcopal tradition—need to hear the voice of the Church of England. After all, we are called to honor our father and mother, and where would Methodism be without its Anglican mother? In this age when theological judgment is so frightfully difficult, the history and tradition and liturgy of this parent church have much to offer us. To take just one example: here, south of the border, we make much of religious experience. But there are some things that should not have to be learned from experience. The richness of our Anglican heritage can remind us of this.

Second, there is Dr. Douglas John Hall, professor at McGill University in Montreal, author, and former student of Paul Tillich. His book, *Lighten Our Darkness*, sounds like a voice of realistic truth crying in a pious wilderness. For example:

> The test of theological authenticity is whether we can present Jesus as the crucified. To be concrete: can one perceive in the Jesus of this theology a man who knows the meaning of meaninglessness, the experience of negation, the anguish of hopelessness? Does he encounter the absurd, and with trembling? Would a man dare to confess to this Jesus his deepest anxieties, his most ultimate questions? Would such a Jesus comprehend the gnawing care of a generation of parents who live every day with the questions: Will my children be able to survive as human beings? . . . Will there be enough to eat? Will they be permitted to have children? Would he, the God-Man of this theology, be able to weep over the dead bodies of little children in Southeast Asia and Brazil, as he wept over his friend Lazarus? . . . Would he be able to agonize over the millions of other beings—not quite little-children, fetuses—for whom there was no place; and over the mothers . . . Could he share our doubt: doubt about

God, about man, about life, about every absolute? Could he understand why we cling to expectations that are no longer affirmed or confirmed by experience, why we repress the most essential questions? Would such a Christ understand failure? Could he participate in our failure? Or is he eternally above all that?[2]

Third, there is the United Church. It was formed in 1925 as a union among Methodists, some Presbyterians, Congregationalists, and other Protestant groups. Today it is a church of some two million members (in a country of only thirty million), built out of a combination of Methodist and Presbyterian policy. It is not a church without problems, but for those of us who are still interested in walking a little further down the road toward ecumenism, the experience of the United Church—in both its victories and defeats—offers a glimpse of what our future might be like. Its predecessor denominations, including Methodism, gave up their inheritance for a new future, gave up their name, habits, and protections for the joy of a better future, a church not only with a yesterday but also with a tomorrow.

Canadian tourism commercials entice us to the natural, scenic, and cultural wonders of Canada, our neighbor to the north, *le Europe prochein,* "the world next door." On a dusty, dreamy summer walk, I believe, we have at least three other reasons for interest: Anglicanism, Doug Hall, and the United Church. Take a look.

Maybe this is the beauty of summer, to nourish our souls in the heart and heat of a looming decade of humiliation, with still nine years to go, and to learn from our smaller, little neighbor due north. Sometimes it can be good to fall in love with the soteriology next door, come summer.

You

May the Good and Gracious God, in the beauty of holiness, make of all of us attentive people, simple and true in our virtues of the

2. Hall, *Lighten Our Darkness,* 211–12.

heart, nourishing and nourished in pardon, disciplined by hard (and even bitter) fences of peace, inspired by gracious clouds, billowing, high, and supported all day long by a summer wind, a spirited faith in the face of death, and a bright willingness to continue to journey, travel, learn, and grow. May we find a little summer beauty in the ant, the berry, the fence, the cloud, the breeze, and the neighbor. *The kingdom of heaven is like a treasure hidden in a field.*

Let Freedom Ring!

Matthew 16:1–4

Monday, July 12th, 2004

University United Methodist Church, Syracuse

Salt and Flowers

There is a dark temptation in the assumption that the cause of freedom is really in the hands of somebody else, someone other than you and me. It is reassuring, too, to judge that the real big advances in liberty have been, are, or will be the work of somebody else.

Today, we want to remember that the history of our region tells another story. Our area was populated by people who saw the expanding circle of freedom as their own responsibility. With Niebuhr, they defined love as taking responsibility.

One of our dear friends has moved to the Southeastern jurisidiction. He joins the ranks of many former parishioners whom we have diligently prepared for their later membership in the Southern United Methodist Church. I celebrate the strong growth of our church in the south. One conference, the North Georgia conference, has more members than our whole Western jurisdiction. One district, East Dallas, has more members than our whole WNY annual conference. I take pleasure and pride in Southern growth. I do so, in part, because you and I have had a hand in it.

As we start our tenth year in ministry here in Rochester, I look back twenty-seven years, at all the folks who have gone south.

Baptized in the ice and snow of North Franklin county; pardoned and delivered of sin in the Adirondack outback; confirmed and strengthened in the faith along the Mohawk; given and taken in marriage by the great Finger Lakes; taught the Scripture and the importance of stewardship on the shores of Lake Ontario; trained and corrected in leadership in the hardy toughness of the Tug Hill plateau; convinced to tithe by the example of northern families who have many winters on the back; and then, sent to retirement in Tampa to die, be buried, and leave their estate to the Florida Annual Conference! Let me tell you the secret of success in growing Southern United Methodist churches: retired Yankees. Where would the Southeast jurisdiction be without all my former parishioners? The secret of southern success? Northern retirees!

Our friend is one such. I playfully commiserated with him about moving to Virginia. How could a Michigander do so? "Oh, it is not a problem any more, Bob. Things have changed. I mean, the South is a different place. And you can take some of the credit."

"Yes, I know, I have marched many Methodists due South over the course of twenty-seven years and seven pulpits. They owe me. We bore, baptized, confirmed, communed, taught, shaped, disciplined, and directed them—and they all went South to leave their estates to the Florida Annual Conference. Here is the secret of Southern growth: retired Yankees."

"No, that's not what I mean. I mean you and others from Syracuse and Rochester have everything to do with it. The new South owes everything to your two home cities!"

"You mean the Salt City and Flower City? The salt of the earth and the lilies of the field?"

"Exactly."

"I am very glad to take the credit, but I just do not know what you mean."

"I mean this. The South is a different place than it was fifty years ago. Totally different, and the difference comes from Rochester and Syracuse. Two things have completed changed the Southern jurisdiction: civil rights and air conditioning! Civil Rights from Rochester and air conditioning from Syracuse!"

Faith and Freedom Along the Erie Canal

The story of air conditioning we leave for another day, though we could use some more right here on a day like today.

Our region bears the distinction of having given rise to many women and men who did not leave freedom to somebody else. Its price of eternal vigilance they provided in very daily, very personal, very local, and very immediate ways. In the same manner by which we take Niagara Falls—so close and so grand—for granted, we take these mighty stories for granted, saving stories of freedom and faith.

We live in the land of Hiawatha ("who causes rivers to run"). Such musical names adorn our home: Canandaigua, Tioghnioga, Onondaga, Tuscarora, Cuyahoga. In the fifteenth century, the great native leader of the Iroquois showed the critical need for union, for space and time in which to live together. His leadership was focused on common space, on collegial relations, on counsel together, and so he is harbinger of all the examples of faith and freedom to come up along the Mohawk and the Erie Canal:

> All your strength is in your union
> All your weakness in discord
> Therefore be at peace henceforward
> And as brothers live together.[1]

This is the land of Harriet Tubman. You may want to visit her home in Auburn. Her neighbor, William Seward, also from Auburn, bought Alaska, considered at the time a folly, an "icebox." Our twenty-first-century theological issue is space. Tubman's grand niece, Janet Lauerson, was on my church staff for a time here on Euclid Avenue, after we both migrated down from the far north country, not far from the burial place of John Brown. His body lies moldering under a ski lift near Lake Placid. He and Gerrit Smith, founder of Peterboro, a short thirty minutes Southeast of your current seat, were not compatibilists regarding slavery. As Lincoln would later say, they felt those who most affirmed slavery

---

1. Longfellow, "Song of Hiawatha," 466.

should start by trying it for themselves. In my childhood, Peterboro, a small village of people of color, stood out as a beachhead of freedom under its civil war statue, one hundred years later. Brown, Smith, Seward, and others were the chorus before which Tubman could sing out the life of freedom, following the underground railroad. Remember her wisdom:

> When I found I had crossed that line, I looked at my hands to see if I was the same person. *There was such a glory over everything* . . . I started with this idea in my head, "There's two things I've got a right to . . . death or liberty" . . . 'Twant me, 'twas the Lord. I always told him, "I trust you. I don't know where to go or what to do, but I expect you to lead me," and he always did.[2]

You will expect to hear something of Frederick Douglass, buried in Rochester. Our cemetery is across the street from our famed Strong Hospital. As one patient said, looking through the window, "It gives you something to think about." Douglass printed the *North Star* in Rochester, and through it, developed a voice for a new people in a new era. At Syracuse University, it was Professor Roland Wolseley who developed the first national program in Black Journalism. Wolseley was formed in the faith under the great preaching of the best Methodist preacher in the twentieth century, Ernest Freemont Tittle, when Wolseley's young wife was Tittle's secretary. I think you should look in the Carrier Dome at the moving tribute to Ernie Davis, a kid from Elmira, who, a century after Douglass, and in the lifespan of Wolseley, gave tragic, courageous, and lasting embodiment to the upstate hope of racial justice, harmony, and integration. He also played football. The voice of Douglass rings out against the harmonic background of Tittle, Wolseley, Davis, and others. In the *North Star*, Douglass wrote: "The whole history of the progress of human liberty shows that all concessions yet made to her august claims have been born of earnest struggle . . . If there is no struggle, there is no progress. Those who profess to favor freedom, and yet deprecate agitation,

2. Tubman, "To Sarah H. Bradford," 523.

are men who want crops without plowing up ground, they want rain without thunder and lightning. They want the ocean without the awful roar of its mighty waters."[3] Or maybe we should give the honor to his cohort, Sojourner Truth: "[Man] says women can't have as many rights as man cause Christ wasn't a woman. Where did your Christ come from? From God and a woman. Man had nothing to do with him!"[4]

Susan B. Anthony did not leave the project of freedom to others. I wonder what sort of dinner companion she might have been. Her constant consort with governors and senators across the Empire state made her an early Eleanor Roosevelt. My grandmother grew up in Cooperstown and graduated from Smith College four years before she had the right to vote. My mother was born in Syracuse only a few years after full suffrage. My wife is a musician and teacher, my sister is a corporate attorney, and my colleagues in ministry are female. I scratch my head to imagine a world without their voices. Syracuse produced Betty Bone Schiess, one of the first women ordained to ministry in the Protestant Episcopal church. One of the Philadelphia Eleven. We study her in our Lemoyne college "Introduction to Religion." One rainy day, when my daughter Emily was 13 and had the flu, we met Schiess, at the druggist. The pharmacist called her name. I clamored over to investigate whether it were she, the famous Schiess. "Who wants to know?" she replied. As she left, after good banter, she turned in her slicker and, totting an umbrella, pronounced this blessing: "One day you will be a Methodist bishop." Thank you, my daughter replied. You may visit the birthplace of suffrage and feminism in Seneca Falls. Anthony's witness stands out among the witness of so many others: your grandmother, your mother, your sister, your wife, your daughter, your pastor, Betty Bone Schiess, and so many others. Who can forget the motto of Susan B. Anthony: "Failure is impossible" (on her eighty-sixth birthday, 1906). "Cautious, careful people, always casting about to preserve their reputation and social standing, never can bring about reform. Those who are

3. Douglass, "Speech at Canandaigua," 509.
4. Truth, "Speech at Woman's Rights Convention," 443.

really in earnest must be willing to be anything or nothing in the world's estimation."[5]

Sometimes the freedom train derailed. Exuberance can produce minor collisions. When we get so focused on the speedometer that we forget to drive the car safely, then trouble arises. I want to talk to you about sexual experimentation, that is, a long time before the summer of love. Woodstock pales by comparison with the communal experiments in our region during the nineteenth century. The Shaker Community and the Oneida Community can perhaps bracket our discussion. Under Mother Ann Lee, and starting in farm country near New Lebanon (Albany area), the shaking Quakers firmly addressed the matter of sex. They forbade it. Like the desert fathers and Qumran communities of old, they took Paul at his word and meditated fully on 1 Corinthians 7. Women and men came together only once a week, on Sunday morning, for ecstatic singing and dancing, hence their name. This made church attendance somewhat more than casual, liturgical observance. However, the practice did not amplify the community itself: infant baptisms lacked the requisite infant, and so were infrequent. Consequently, the Shakers moved to Cleveland, where they blended into Sherwood Anderson's new Ohio, returning to the old ways of hard work, monogamy, and frugality. In short, they became Methodists. Here again the Shaker tune:

> *Tis a gift to be loving*
> *Tis the best gift of all*
> *Like a gentle rain love falls to cover all*
> *When we find ourselves in the place just right*
> *'Twill be in the valley of love and delight*
> *When true, simplicity is gain*
> *To bow and to bend we shan't be ashamed*
> *To turn, turn, will be our delight*
> *'Till by turning, turning, we come round right.*[6]

5. Anthony, "On the Campaign for Divorce Law Reform," 521.
6. Brackett, "'Tis the Gift to be Simple."

Now, the Oneidas. You may want to read Spencer Klaw's *Without Sin*, the best selling review of their somewhat different experiment.[7] Just a few miles East of here, the Oneida community set out to find heaven on earth, the end of all oppressions, and even the hope that, as John H. Noyes read from Revelation, "Death itself will be no more." Although I went to High School in Oneida, I do not recall a full lesson on the matter of stirpiculture, the heart of the Oneida experiment. Due to new technology, our own time approaches the horizon of a new eugenics. Ask any pregnant couple about the number of tests available today and what choices they must make. The Oneidas practiced "complex" marriage, in which every man was married to every woman (and vice-versa) and sexual relations were freely permitted as long as the men practiced "continence" to avoid pregnancy. Procreation was planned, through a deliberated committee process, but nonetheless they also practiced free-love sharing of the marriage bed in the hope of producing a better race, a finer human being. (For those of you for whom this is more information than you require, I apologize.) Three hundred in number at their greatest growth, the community produced bear traps and then silver, continuing, in some fashion, to this day. Of all the utopian experiments, the Oneida project is the most fascinating. After word got out about the doings and practices in Oneida, clergy in Syracuse banded together and ran them out of town, first to Canada and then to the Midwest. Noyes died on the trip, and the community disappeared, except on your dinner table, in wedding gifts, and in quality restaurants. Let us remember the love of freedom, as Noyes expressed it, even if we cannot affirm his methods: "I am free of sin and in a state of Perfection."

I conclude this pastiche with an unlikely name. When we were at Union Seminary in New York, the faculty there, both regularly and rightly criticized the inadequate theology of the Marble Collegiate Church. I remember James Sanders sternly referring to this famed congregation as the "First Church of Marduke," not an accolade. Of course you know that, for fifty years, a graduate of

7. See Klaw, *Without Sin*.

Ohio Wesleyan and a proponent of the power of positive thinking held forth, without notes, from the Marduke pulpit. His son
in law, Arthur Caliandro, does so today, with notes. You may not
trust his theology. I myself am a critic, schooled as I was in the
dour, German realism of Tillich, Niehbuhr, and company. You
may find it too shallow. Everbody has their criticism of Norman
Vincent Peale. Even Adlai Stevenson had gripes. When attacked
from Marduke, Stevenson defended his Christianity on the basis
of the Apostle to the Gentiles, all this in 1956, and rounded out his
peroration thus: "Sir, I find Paul appealing, but Peale, appalling."[8]
You, too, may find Paul appealing and Peale appalling. But hold
one thought. Peale preached right here. I mean right here. In Syracuse University Church. He found a happy people here. He found a
positive people here. He found a hopeful people here, an optimistic
congregation. Why, they were so good to him, he relaxed and fell
in love and married an SU coed, Ruth. Forrest Whitmeyer knew
them both well. It was that native-buckeye spirit married to that
native-orange soul, and it produced the power of positive thinking,
itself a form of faith and freedom not to be forgotten. The Peales,
Ruth and Norman both, did not leave the project of freedom to
somebody else. It is biblical and faithful to remember Peale's seven
most important words: "You can if you think you can."

A Sign of the Times

God was in Christ, reconciling the world to himself. The faith of
Jesus Christ and the freedom of Jesus Christ we celebrate today.
Our forebears were disinclined to leave the pursuit of freedom to
others. They seized freedom in their own hands and by their own
lives. They did not wait on others. They did not pause to seek a secret blessing. They did not wait until some ethereal sign emerged.
They did not expect some magic insight. They preferred deliverance to discernment. And it is their love of freedom that is our
greatest remembrance across this region.

8. As said during his unsuccessful campaign for President, 1956.

We close with Jesus' warning. The clergy and lay leadership (scribes and Pharisees) came seeking a sign. This is the only place in the New Testament in which the word "discernment" is used (with one technical exception, in 1 Cor 11). They seek some higher, Gnostic insight, some discernment. They want to figure things out ahead of time. They want to know how to judge, to pull apart, to discern. They want a spiritual elixir. Who wouldn't? What one of us has not looked for a sign? It is as natural a religious sentiment as one can imagine.

How staggering, startling, then, is Jesus condemnatory response. In the one appearance of "discernment" in his teaching, Jesus roundly rejects such an approach. He senses a retreat from real life, a fleeing from freedom, a hiding out from history—perhaps an apocalyptic gone bad. Did you hear his response? You need no more signs than the morning and evening sky. We have the same folklore: "Red sky in morning, sailors take warning." No, you know how to read nature, and you can just as easily read history. Poverty unabated means revolution to come. The greatest cause of war is war. 1 percent of the people holding 50 percent of the wealth means trouble. Justice delayed is justice denied. You need no sign, just read the signs of the times. You get only the sign of Jonah, that prophetic exemplar of universal deliverance, global freedom. No sign. Fussing with discernment is avoiding deliverance. Real love is taking historical responsibility.

Your Declaration of Independence

In earshot of our Lord's teaching, in remembrance of the freedom and faith in this region, and especially on this happy day, there is no avoiding a very personal question: as a Christian man or woman, what are you going to do to continue to expand the circle of freedom in our time? Where is your tribal council to create? Where is your slavery to escape? Where is your North Star to publish? Where is your franchise to find? Where is your libertinism to avoid? Where is your hope to share? Are you to celebrate independence by singing and smiling only? Is discernment all you care about? Or will you lift a hand?

> *Give me your tired, your poor*
> *Your huddled masses yearning to breath free*
> *The restless refuse of your teeming shore*
> *Send these, the lost, the tempest tossed to me*
> *I lift my lamp beside the golden door.*[9]

---

9. This citation from Emma Lazarus is found on the Statue of Liberty.

Persistence in Prayer

Luke 18:9–19
Sunday, October 23rd, 2016
Family and Friends (Parents) Weekend
Marsh Chapel at Boston University

Yeats in Poetic Prayer

(for confession)

Turning and turning in the widening gyre
The falcon cannot hear the falconer;
Things fall apart; the centre cannot hold;
Mere anarchy is loosed upon the world,
The blood-dimmed tide is loosed, and everywhere
The ceremony of innocence is drowned;
The best lack all conviction, while the worst
Are full of passionate intensity.[1]

Persistence in prayer is difficult, in our age.

Prayer in Luke

We can readily appreciate the stark rigor of Jesus' Lukan parables: a Samaritan whose kindness illumines the limits of religion; a rich man, who builds bigger barns, but whose soul

1. Yeats, "Michael Robartes and the Dancer," 639.

suddenly is required; a figure of a fig tree, fruitless, but spared for yet another year in hope; a marriage feast wherein humility is tested and the poor are fed; another banquet to which many are invited but few respond, and out to highways and byways the invitation goes; a lost sheep—found!; a lost coin—found!; a lost, prodigal son—found!; a truly dishonest steward whose wiliness shines out; a rich man, who turns his back on a poor man, and roasts in hell for it; a persistent widow, who raises her voice to an unjust judge; talent wasted and invested; a vineyard stolen by tenants; and, today, a publican persistent in prayer.

What drove Luke, alone, to remember or construct these parables? The lengthening years, without ultimate victory, since the cross? The long decades of living without Jesus? The uncertainties of institution and culture and citizenship and multiple responsibilities? The daily stresses of managing a budget? It is the primitive church that can give an example for us today in our time of anxiety. They waited for Jesus to return. And he delayed. And he delays, still. It is enough to make you lose heart.

> Though with a scornful wonder we see her sore oppressed
> By schism rent asunder by heresy distressed
> Yet saints their watch are keeping their cry goes up 'howlong'?
> And soon the night of weeping will be the morn of song.

Persistence in prayer takes faith, to be in faith.

The publican—the tax collector—looks hard into the mirror. *God be merciful to me—a sinner!* He uses a word that we avoid. Sin is utterly personal. This we understand. The covenantal commands of the decalogue have a personal consequence (Exod 20). As grace touches ground in Jesus Christ, sin touches sand in personal confessions. We get lost. It is our nature, East of eden. We get lost in sex without love: lust. We get lost in consumption without nourishment: gluttony. We get lost in accumulation without investment: avarice. We get lost in rest without weariness, in happiness without struggle: sloth. We get lost in righteousness without restraint: anger. We get lost in desire without ration or respect: envy. And most regularly, we get lost in integrity without humility: pride. If you have never known lust, gluttony, avarice, sloth, anger, envy, or pride, you are not a sinner, you are outside the cloud of sin, and you need no repentance. (You also may not be quite human.)

It is a long wait. And that is just the point. Like the bridesmaids who waited with lamps trimmed, we feel the length of the wait. But we can wait together. We can offer together a common prayer. We can slowly, stumblingly give ourselves over to persistence in prayer, to the forms of religious practice that bear meaning, to the life of the church, for all its foibles, wherein we learn the grammar of grace, and wherethrough we face down the evils of this age.

Persistence in prayer is challenging, in our tradition.

Techne

Virginia Woolf's serious joke that "on or about December 1910, human character changed" was a hundred years premature. Human character changed on or about December 2010, when everyone, it seemed, started carrying a smartphone. For the first time, practically anyone could be found intruded upon, not only at some fixed address at home or at work, but everywhere at all times. Before this, everyone could expect, in the course of the day, some time at least in which to be left alone, unobserved, unsustained, and unburdened by public or familial roles. That era now came to an end.

When the smartphone brings messages, alerts, and notifications that invite instant responses—and induces anxiety if those messages fail to arrive—everyone's sense of time changes, and attention that used to be focused more or less distantly on, say, tomorrow's mail is concentrated in the present moment . . . You cannot reduce your engagement with the past and future without diminishing yourself, without becoming "more tenuous."[2]

Persistence in prayer is challenging, in our culture.

---

2. Mendelson, "In the Depths of the Digital Age."

Rather than another hour of email or on our smartphone, perhaps we could walk, alone, quiet, and talk to God. Tell it to God. Pray. Our overcapacity in email is a direct consequence of our underinvestment in prayer.

Prayer in Life: Charles Taylor

One advantage of a life of study, the life of the mind, the college years, is the chance to pick out some new theological eyeglasses. Prayerfully consider, for example, the thought of Charles Taylor, our Montreal philosopher. Taylor explores background conditions: social imaginaries, moral perspectives, the cultural influences we sometimes take for granted. His central emphasis is the exploration of "fullness": an experience of what counts most in life. Taylor views the spiritual shape of the present age through the lenses of the work of Ivan Illich, Charles Peguy, G. M. Hopkins, and Isaiah Berlin. He has no interest in a return to an untroubled harmony, which is utterly unattainable and even a kind of culpable weakness. Taylor seeks a new more nuanced map of the ideological terrain all about us. Fullness . . .

I prayerfully remember the summer, thinking, in prayer, of Taylor. When I see my granddaughter, Ellie, tubing behind a motor boat for the first time, I have the joyful fullness of watching her as a remembrance of her mother, our daughter, Emily skiing on the same lake. When our youngest granddaughter, Hannah, wakes up from a nap; or when her brother Charlie, "screwing his courage to the sticking post," tries tubing himself; or when their cousin Sally cries out wanting her dad, our son, Benjamin; or when Jan comes home as happy as Yogi Bear, her bucket full of blackberries; or when the blue lake and blue sky outside our blue cottage call out the name of the Blue God; then there is fullness, in a summer hue.

Charles Taylor, a great Canadian, has something he rails against: subtraction (of transcendence) theories. That is, he fights against the late modern urge to bracket out such transcendence. Transcendence in ordinary life, in society, in erotic love, in a new poetic language—Taylor works to make sufficient cultural space for transcendence. That is what we are about at Marsh Chapel, too. Taylor affirms not disenchantment but re-enchantment: claims for belief, for God, a sense of the soul and salvation, over against the modern or late modern experience of malaise, ennui, uncertainty, meaninglessness, melancholy, and despair. Here is his question: "Where in the culture of expressive individualism is the sacred?" To this end, Taylor examines a kind of "diffusive Christianity," a habit of moving between belief and unbelief, an emphasis on believing, not belonging. His work heralds a new age of religious searching—not a decline in religious belief and practice but rather a plurality of forms of belief and unbelief, transitory and fragile, existing within a range of cross pressures within the ongoing contest of religiosity and materialism. He criticizes what he calls "excarnation" (a shift from taking the body seriously, head over other). In all, Taylor is the evangelist for the joy of everyday relationships, conduct, and experiences, his ear tuned to the sacred, his eye searching out the range of the sacred canopy, his mind alive to spirit, his heart given over to a hymnic celebration of our aspiration to wholeness. His work is a hymn to and of persistence in prayer.[3]

We fear—and try to find our security in larger automobiles, drug supplies, stock collections, homes, or layers of disconnection, gated communities of the mind and heart. And yet, security does not come through possession but through relationship. Do you want to be safe and secure? Invest yourself in a lifetime of building and keeping healthy relationships. There is your security, where neither moth nor rust consumes.

Such persistence in prayer needs new theological eyes, in our era.

Persistence in Prayer

Ernest Fremont Tittle was the greatest Methodist preacher of his mid-twentieth-century generation. Tougher than Sockman, truer

---

3. Charles Taylor, in conversation with Philip Amerson, Robert Allan Hill, and Michael Morgan, Indiana University.

than Peale, Tittle preached in Chicago until he died at his desk, writing about Luke:

> There is special need for persistence in prayer when the object sought is the redressing of social wrongs. God will see justice done if the human instruments of his justice do not give way to weariness, impatience, or discouragement, but persevere in prayer and labor for the improvement of world conditions. Here we can learn from the scientist. Medical research is a prayer for the relief of suffering, the abolition of disease, the conservation of life—a prayer in which the scientist perseveres in the face of whatever odds, whatever darkness and delay. More especially, we can learn from great religious leaders like Luther, Wesley, Wilberforce, and Shaftsbury, who year upon year prayed and fought for the causes to which they dedicated their lives. The need for persistence in prayer arises not only from the intransigence of the oppressor, but also from the immaturity and imperfection of the would-be reformer. We have a lot to learn and much in ourselves to overcome before we can be used of God as instruments of his justice. Recognizing this, Gandhi spent hours each day in prayer and meditation, and maintained a weekly day of silence.[4]

Persistence in prayer takes practice, for those who seek to resist injustice.

A Common Prayer

We offer a common prayer, a prayer that our warming globe, caught in climate change, will be cooled by cooler heads and calmer hearts and careful minds.

We offer a common prayer, a prayer that our dangerous world, armed to the teeth with nuclear proliferation, will find peace through deft leadership toward nuclear détente.

---

4. Tittle, *Gospel According to Luke*, 190.

We offer a common prayer, a prayer that our culture, awash in part in hooliganism, will find again the language and the song and the spirit of the better angels of our nature.

We offer a common prayer, a prayer that our country, fractured by massive inequality between rich children and poor children, will rise up and make education, free education, available to all children, poor and rich.

We offer a common prayer, a prayer that our nation, fractured by flagrant unjust inequality between rich and poor children, will stand up and make health care, free health care, available to all children, poor and rich.

We offer a common prayer, a prayer that our schools, colleges and universities, will balance a love of learning with a sense of meaning, a pride in knowledge with a respect for goodness, a drive for discovery with a regard for recovery.

We offer a common prayer, a prayer that our families, torn apart by abuse and distrust and anger and jealousy and unkindness, will sit at a long Thanksgiving table, this autumn, and share the turkey and pass the potatoes, and slice the pie, and, if grudgingly, show kindness and pity to one another.

We offer a common prayer, a prayer that our decisions in life about our callings, how we are to use our time and spend our money, how we make a life not just a living, will be illumined by grace and generosity.

We offer a common prayer, a prayer that our grandfathers and mothers, in their age and infirmity, will receive care and kindness that accords with the warning to honor father and mother that you own days be long upon the earth.

We offer a common prayer, a prayer that women—our grandmothers, mothers, sisters, daughters, granddaughters, all—granted suffrage less than one hundred years ago, will be spared any and all forms of harassment and abuse, verbal or physical, on college campuses, in homes and families, in offices and bars, in life and work, and long-having suffered and now-having suffrage, will, in our time, rise up to be honored, revered, and compensated, without reserve, but with justice and mercy.

We offer a common prayer, finally a prayer not of this world, but of this world as a field of formation for another, not just creation but new creation, not just life but eternal life, not just health but salvation, not just heart but soul, and not just earth but heaven.

Application in Prayer

Talk to God walking on the river, in the woods, on the beach, once a day—do not use email and other such modes when a silent prayer will suffice.

Go to church once a week, for sermon and music and eucharist, but also to see different others, to feel different neighbors, to place yourself in the community of God's people.

Give away 10 percent of what you earn, to the church you love, to the mission you admire, to the school that taught you, to the place where help meets hurt.

Read. When you read, read every sentence and think it through. Read your Bible. Read a good newspaper. Read.

What shall we say? How shall we pray?

> Labor Omnia Vincit
> Do not lose heart
> Work conquers all
> Pray always
> All of us are better when we are loved
> Do not lose heart
> Early to bed and early to bed and early to rise
> Pray always
> A stitch in time
> Do not lose heart
> Waste not want not
> Pray always
> Rome was not built in a day
> Do not lose heart
> Only the devil has no time
> To let things grow
> Pray always

Persistence in prayer begins with a decision to pray "without ceasing."

God be merciful to me, a sinner. I tell you, this man went down to his home justified.[5]

5. Luke 18:13–14.

Come Down Zacchaeus!

Luke 19:1–10
Sunday, October 30th, 2016
Reformation Sunday
Marsh Chapel at Boston University

Did we in our own strength confide
Our striving would be losing
Were not the Right Man on our side
The Man of God's own choosing
Dost as who that may be?
Christ Jesus it is He
Lord Sabaoth His name
From age to age the same
And he must win the battle.[1]

It is hard for me to tell, from this angle, which tree you are in. Given the troubles of this autumn, it is hard for me to tell which tree I am in myself, day to day. Has life chased you up the tree of doubt? Or are you treed in the branches of idolatry—idol-a-tree? Are we shaking (or shaking in) the money tree? Or stuck without

1. Luther, "Mighty Fortress," 110.

faith in the religion tree? Jesus calls us today, to come down out of the treeforts of our own making, and accept a loving relationship with Him. May we measure all with a measure of love.

Doubting Zacchaeus

Perhaps the presence of unexplained wrong provokes you to doubt the benevolence in life or the goodness in God. To doubt that "God is at work in the world to make and to keep human life human."[2] Randomness may have treed you.

No one can explain why terrible things happen as they do. But if you will come down a limb or two from your philosophical tree of doubt, the tree of the knowledge of good and evil, you may hear faith. God can bring good out of evil, and make bad things work to good. This is not a theological declamation, and certainly not a paean to providence. It is just something we can notice together.

We played golf one day. On the last hole, I pulled out a three wood and hit a grounder that, nonetheless, rolled right to the green. If I had connected, I would have smashed the clubhouse window, for it was way too much club. Sometimes a bad thing, a worm-burner golf shot, interferes with a really bad thing—a $1000 broken window.

One Sunday, years ago, I drove late to church. I used to run early Sunday and finish memorizing the sermon along the way, as I did on that Lord's Day. I just forgot the time. We raced to church and, in so doing, I cut a corner, literally, and popped a car tire. I was not happy to hear my son say, "Haste makes waste." You know, though, both rear tires were thin. I had replaced the front two months earlier and forgot about the rear ones. I have to admit, it was good that I had reason to replace them, before I had a blowout on the highway. Sometimes it happens that a bad thing prevents a really terrible thing from happening.

Joseph was thrown into a pit and sold into slavery. He had to find his way, as a Jew, in the service of the mighty Pharaoh.

2. John Bennett, as recalled by his students, in conversation.

He did so with skill and rose to a position of influence, even with Potiphar's wife chasing him around in his underwear. Then, a full generation later, a great famine came upon those brothers who had earlier sold Joseph down the river. They went to Pharaoh, looking for food. And who met them, as they came to plead? There was Joseph. He so memorably said, as written in Genesis: "You meant this for evil, but God meant it for good, that many might be saved" (Gen 50:20). Sometimes it happens that a bad thing in one generation prevents starvation in the next.

So in Jericho, as Jesus found the little man up in the tree, his fellows grumbled (Luke 19:8). Why would he take time with such a greedy, selfish person, who makes his living off the sweat of others' brows? That hurts, to see divine attention given to those who have harmed you. Why would he have a meal with someone who takes no thought for the hurt of God's people? This is bad! And it is. We miss the power of the parable if we do not see this. This is Jesus taking up with those who have wished the church ill, who have used the church for their own very well intended but nonetheless self-centered reasons. This is Jesus consorting with sinners. But sometimes a bad thing in the little brings a good thing in the large. Zacchaeus changes and, in so doing, provides great wealth for others' benefit.

Come down from this one tree, doubting Zacchaeus. I know that bad things happen to good people and, as a pastor, hardly anything troubles me more. Sometimes, though, sometimes—not always, just sometimes—a bad thing early averts a really bad thing late. I have seen it and you have too. It is enough to give someone up the doubting tree a reason to come down at least a branch. Think of it as existential vaccination.

It is the labor of faith to trust that where sin abounds, grace over-abounds. Even in this autumn of anxiety and depression. But one of the redeeming possibilities in this season of cultural demise is the chance that, as a result, enough of us, now, will become committed to the realization of a just, participatory, and sustainable world, that these darker days will move us toward a fuller light.

Sometimes a bad thing in one part of history protects us from a worse thing in another part.

Let us not lose sight of the horizons of biblical hope, as improbable as they can seem. The lion and the lamb. No crying or thirst. The crooked straight. All flesh.

The divine delight still comes from saving the lost, including the forgotten, seeking the outcast, retrieving the wayward sons and daughters of Abraham. God wants your salvation. Your salvation "has personal, domestic, social, and economic consequences."[3] Jesus Christ saves us from doubt.

So come down, Zacchaeus, come down from your perch in that comfortable sycamore tree, that comfortable pew, that skeptical reserve, that doubt. Come down, Zacchaeus! The Lord Jesus Christ has need of your household and your money, and He responds to your doubt.

Idolatrous Zacchaeus

Come down, Zacchaeus, down from your overly zealous leanings, hanging out on the branch of life. Idolatry comes when we make one or more of the lesser, though significant, loyalties in life to become a shadow of the one great loyalty, that which the heart alone owes to God. Zacchaeus had governmental responsibility, community status, a welcoming home, and a fine family; we can suspect he was loyal in these regards. Curious as he was, up on his branch, he had no relationship with the divine. Jesus invites him into this relationship. More precisely, Jesus invites himself into relationship with a man up a tree. He is invited into a whole new life, a new world of loving and faithful relationships that stem from the one great loyalty.

We need to be careful about lesser loyalties this fall.

Remember last week and our prayer for forgiveness of sin? We confessed lust, gluttony, avarice, sloth, anger, envy, and "integrity without humility"—pride. Say you were an attorney general in

3. Fred Craddock, in personal conversation. First Baptist Church, Rochester, New York, 2001.

a state with a governor's election ten days away. You find a folder on your desk, empty, but with a pending potential investigation. You feel that your integrity requires that you tell the whole inhabited earth about a pending possible investigation about which you know nothing. You remember your Boy Scout law (trustworthy, loyal, helpful, friendly, courteous, kind, obedient, cheerful, thrifty, brave, clean, and reverent), and decide your integrity requires a statement. But what of your humility? (The scout motto—a good turn daily—not just the law.) Humility would require you to consider due process, to consider past practice near elections, to consider the advice of your colleagues in law enforcement, and to consider the nuances of the situation and your conscience. Integrity alone bulldozes, blazes, and blasts past all these. Harm is done. Integrity without humility is the worst of the seven deadly sins— pride. When we grow up, sometimes, we recognize the peril of integrity alone, the great steed of integrity, without the bit, bridle, and saddle of humility—pride.

Yet all of this involves a lesser loyalty than the one owed to God. If we are not careful, we can forget whose water we were baptized into. Rather, let us remember the student of Paul who wrote in 2 Thessalonians: "Your faith is growing abundantly, and the love of every one of you for one another is increasing" (2 Thess 1: 4).

Do you see the danger? Come down, Zacchaeus, come down, before it is too late. Make sure your lesser loyalties—to government, family, home, and all—do not cover over, do not shadow the one great loyalty, that all of your daily tasks do not eclipse a living memory of a common dream:

We harbor a common dream, a dream that our warming globe, caught in climate change, will be cooled by cooler heads and calmer hearts and careful minds.

We harbor a common dream, a dream that our dangerous world, armed to the teeth with nuclear proliferation, will find peace through deft leadership toward nuclear détente.

We harbor a common dream, a dream that our culture, awash in part in hooliganism, will find again the language and the song and the spirit of the better angels of our nature.

We harbor a common dream, a dream that our country, fractured by massive inequality between rich children and poor children, will rise up and make education, free education, available to all children, poor and rich.

We harbor a common dream, a dream that our nation, fractured by flagrant, unjust inequality between rich and poor children, will stand up and make health care, free health care, available to all children, poor and rich.

We harbor a common dream, a dream that our schools, colleges and universities, will balance a love of learning with a sense of meaning, a pride in knowledge with a respect for goodness, a drive for discovery with a regard for recovery.

We harbor a common dream, a dream that our families, torn apart by abuse, distrust, anger, jealousy, and unkindness, will sit at a long Thanksgiving table, share the turkey, pass the potatoes, and slice the pie, and, if grudgingly, show kindness and pity to one another.

We harbor a common dream, a dream that our decisions in life about our callings, how we are to use our time and spend our money, how we make a life not just a living, will be illumined by grace and generosity.

We harbor a common dream, a dream that our grandfathers and mothers, in their age and infirmity, will receive care and kindness that accords with the warning to honor father and mother that your own days be long upon the earth.

We harbor a common dream, a dream that women—our grandmothers, mothers, sisters, daughters, granddaughters, and all—granted suffrage less than one hundred years ago, will be spared any and all forms of harassment and abuse, verbal or physical, on college campuses, in homes and families, in offices and bars, in life and work, and long having suffered and now having suffrage, will, in our time, rise up to be honored, revered, and compensated, without reserve, but with justice and mercy.

We harbor a common dream, finally, a dream not of this world but of this world as a field of formation for another, not just creation but new creation, not just life but eternal life, not just health but salvation, not just heart but soul, not just earth but heaven.

Wealthy Zacchaeus

Come down, Zacchaeus, come down, at last. Impediments to faith come through doubt, idolatry, resentment, and religion, but none of these holds a candle to the harm that wealth can bring. In global and historical terms, every one of us in this room is wealthy. Our problems are first-world problems. Luke's entire gospel, especially its central chapters, is aimed at this point. For Luke's community, the remembered teachings of Jesus about wealth were most important. That tells me that the Lukan church had money, and so do we. This is what makes the account of Zacchaeus, "one who lined his own pockets at other people's expense," so dramatic for Luke, and so Luke concludes his travel narrative with this clarion call: come down. Be careful as you do not to trip over wealth, power, or health. We lose them all, give them all away, over time. They are 'impermanences'. They go. Better that we see so early. *Time flies— ah no. Time stays—we go.*

Wouldn't you love to know what Jesus said to Zacchaeus that caused him to give away half of what he had? I would.

It is a western, white, educated, wealthy, healthy, heterosexual, middle class, two handed, male world. I need to be reminded of that. Come down Zaccheus, and feel the pain of others. And: Soon we will all be dead. Maybe we could find ways to use whatever power we have now to honor God, love our neighbor, reflect our mortality, and affirm the powerless. Come down, Zacchaeus, come down!

Before we left seminary, on the day after Thanksgiving in 1978, an odd event befell us. In those years, I worked nights as a security guard and would come home to sleep at 7:00 AM. Jan had the day off and left to shop, but left the door to our little apartment ajar by accident. Around noon, a street woman found her way into the building, up into our floor, and then into our room. I woke up to see a very poor, deranged woman, fingering rosary beads and mumbling just over my head. Boy did I shout. She ran into the next room and I stumbled downstairs to call the police. By the time three of New York's finest and I returned to the apartment, the poor lady was in the bathtub, singing and washing. They took her away. Jan came back at 3:00 PM and asked how I had slept. The moment has stayed in the memory, though, as an omen. Our wealth is meant for the cleansing of the poor of the earth. Perhaps the Lord wanted me to remember that in ministry, so I have tried to. Come down, Zacchaeus, and use your wealth for the poor.

Religious Zacchaeus

Let's talk for a moment about religion, shall we? Come down, Zacchaeus, come down! No amount of religious apparatus can ever substitute for what Jesus is offering today, and that is loving relationship. No amount of theological astuteness can ever substitute for loving relationship. No amount of sturdy churchmanship can ever substitute for loving relationship. No amount of righteous indignation can ever substitute for loving relationship. No amount of church music, instrumental or vocal, can ever substitute for loving relationship. No amount of formal religion can ever substitute for the power of loving relationship. Jesus invites us into loving relationship with him, and so with each other. That is salvation. Are we lovers anymore?

Like Zacchaeus in the tree, religion can dwell above Jesus, high and aloof. Is it good to be above Jesus?

It was the German monk, Martin Luther, who, in 1517, went alone and nailed his ninety-five theses to the door in Wittenberg, thereby splintering inherited religion to bits. On a rainy night in London, 1738, along Aldersgate Street, the words of this same Luther were read as an interpretation of Romans 8, as John Wesley's heart, at long last, was strangely warmed, and he came down from the tree of religion to sit at table with the Faith of Christ. We remember Luther this Sunday every year. We pointedly remember that we are saved by faith, by faith alone, by grace we are saved by faith, and not by any or all the works of the law.

Here is an old, ostensibly humorous story. A man approaches the pearly gates. "Tell me about the good in your life," says Peter, "Admission requires 100 points."

"Well, I once gave to the United Way (1 point) . . . and I remember I shoveled a neighbor's walk (1 point) . . . and I used to go to church (1 point)."

Pause.

"You know, I'll never make it to 100 points except by the grace of God."

And Peter replies: "YOU ARE IN THE GRACE OF GOD— THAT'S 97 POINTS!"

Luther recalls us down from the religion tree to sit at the table of faith:

> Sola Fide.
>
> Crux Sola Nostra Theologia.
>
> Sin Boldly, but trust upon the Lord Jesus Christ more boldly still.
>
> In the midst of the affliction He counsels, strengthens, confirms, nourishes, and favors us . . . Moreover, when we have repented, He instantly remits the sins as well as the punishments. In the same manner, parents ought to handle their children.
>
> Thus every matter, if it is to be done well, calls for the attention of the whole person.
>
> If there is anything in us, it is not our own; it is a gift of God. But if it is a gift of God, then it is entirely a debt one owes to love, that is, to the law of Christ. And if it is a debt owed to love, then I must serve others with it, not myself. Thus my learning is not my own; it belongs to the unlearned and is the debt I owe them . . . My wisdom belongs to the foolish, my power to the oppressed. Thus my wealth belongs to the poor, my righteousness to the sinners.
>
> It is with all these qualities that we must stand before God and intervene on behalf of those who do not have them, as though clothed with someone else's garment . . . But even before men we must, with the same love, render them service against their detractors and those who are violent toward them; for this is what Christ did for us.

Teaching is of more importance than urging.

One learns more of Christ in being married and rearing children than in several lifetimes spent in study in a monastery.

One becomes a theologian by living, by dying, and by being damned, not by understanding, reading, and speculation.

What would it profit us to possess and perform everything else and be like pure saints, if we meanwhile neglected our chief purpose in life, namely, the care of the young?

Without a doubt we are named after Christ—not absent from us but dwelling within us; in other words: provided that we believe in him and that, in turn and mutuality, we are a second Christ to one another, doing for our neighbors as Christ does for us.[4]

Come down Zacchaeus! Come down from the doubting tree, the tree of idolatry, the wealth tree, the tree of religion. Come down and receive the Gospel: Jesus invites us into loving relationship with himself, and thereby into loving relationship with our neighbors.

Did we in our own strength confide
Our striving would be losing
Were not the Right Man on our side
The Man of God's own choosing
Dost as who that may be?
Christ Jesus it is He
Lord Sabaoth His name
From age to age the same
And he must win the battle.[5]

---

4. Luther, "Freedom of a Christian," 467–538.
5. Luther, "Mighty Fortress," 110.

Bibliography

Anthony, Susan Brownell. "On the Campaign for Divorce Law Reform, 1860." In *Bartlett's Familiar Quotations*, edited by Justin Kaplan, 521. 17th edition. Boston: Little, Brown, 2002.

Blake, William. "Broken Love." In *The Oxford Book of English Mystical Verse*, edited by Nicholson, et al., 57. Oxford: Clarendon, 1917.

Bonhoeffer, Dietrich. *By Gracious Powers*. Translated by Fred Pratt Green. Nashville: United Methodist, 2000.

Brackett, Joseph. "'Tis the Gift to be Simple." Hymnary.org. https://hymnary.org/text/tis_the_gift_to_be_simple.

Bradbury, Ray. *Fahrenheit 451*. New York: Ballentine, 1953.

Brueggeman, Walter. *Like Fire in the Bones: Listening for the Prophetic Word in Jeremiah*. Minneapolis: Fortress, 2006.

Douglass, Frederick. "Speech at Canandaigua, New York, 1857." In *Bartlett's Familiar Quotations*, edited by Justin Kaplan, 509. 17th edition. Boston: Little, Brown, 2002.

Franklin, Benjamin. "Poor Richard's Almanac, 1735." In *Bartlett's Familiar Quotations*, edited by Justin Kaplan, 319. 17th edition. Boston: Little, Brown, 2002.

Gilmour, S. Maclean. *The Gospel According to St. Luke: Exegesis*. The Interpreters' Bible 8. New York: Abingdon, 1952.

Hammarskjold, Dag. *Markings*. New York: Random House, 2006.

Hirschman, Albert O. *Exit, Voice, and Loyalty*. Cambridge: Harvard University Press, 1970.

Howe, Julia Ward. "Battle Hymn of the Republic." In *United Methodist Hymnal*, 717. Nashville: United Methodist, 2000.

King, Martin Luther, Jr. "Speech at Civil Rights March on Washington." In *Bartlett's Familiar Quotations*, edited by Justin Kaplan, 823. 17th edition. Boston: Little, Brown, 2002.

Lasch, Christopher. *The True and Only Heaven: Progress and its Critics*. New York: Random House, 1991.

Lincoln, Abraham. "Address to an Indiana Regiment." In *Bartlett's Familiar Quotations*, edited by Justin Kaplan, 477. 17th edition. Boston: Little, Brown, 2002.

Lincoln, Abraham. "Second Inaugural Address." In *Bartlett's Familiar Quotations*, edited by Justin Kaplan, 477. 17th edition. Boston: Little, Brown, 2002.

Longfellow, Henry Wadsworth. "Song of Hiawatha, 1855." In *Bartlett's Familiar Quotations*, edited by Justin Kaplan, 466. 17th edition. Boston: Little, Brown, 2002.

Luther, Martin. "The Freedom of a Christian." In *The Roots of Reform*. Vol. 1 of *The Annotated Luther*. Edited by Timothy J. Wengert, 467–538. Minneapolis: Fortress, 2015.

Luther, Martin. "A Mighty Fortress Is Our God." Translated by Frederick Hedge. Nashville: United Methodist, 2000.

Martyn, J. L. "Epistemology at the Turn of the Ages: 2 Cor 5:16." In *Christian History and Interpretation: Studies Presented to John Knox*, edited by W. R. Farmer, et al. Cambridge, 1967.

Mendelson, Edward. "In the Depths of the Digital Age." New York Review of Books. 23 June 2016. https://www.nybooks.com/articles/2016/06/23/depths-of-the-digital-age.

Moore, Thomas. *The Care of the Soul*. New York: Random House.

Poe, Marshall. "Colleges Should Teach Religion to Their Students." The Atlantic. 7 March 2014. https://www.theatlantic.com/education/archive/2014/03/colleges-should-teach-religion-to-their-students/284296.

Proust, Marcel. *Remembrance of Things Past*. 2 vols. Translated by C. K. Scott Moncrieff and Frederick A. Blossom. New York: Random House, 1934.

Rickey, Branch. "Branch Rickey Quotes." AZquotes.com. https://www.azquotes.com/author/12336-Branch_Rickey.

Santayana, George. "The Life of Reason, 1905." In *Bartlett's Familiar Quotations*, edited by Justin Kaplan, 629. 17th edition. Boston: Little, Brown, 2002.

Schulweis, Harold M. "Two Prophets, One Soul." The Shalom Center. 8 September 2001. https://theshalomcenter.org/node/122.

Tittle, Ernest Freemont. *The Gospel According to Luke: Exposition and Application*. New York: Harper and Brothers, 1951.

Truth, Sojourner. "Speech at Woman's Rights Convention, 1851." In *Bartlett's Familiar Quotations*, edited by Justin Kaplan, 443. 17th edition. Boston: Little, Brown, 2002.

Tubman, Harriet. "To Sarah H. Bradford." In *Bartlett's Familiar Quotations*, edited by Justin Kaplan, 523. 17th edition. Boston: Little, Brown, 2002.

Unamuno, Miguel de. "The Tragic Sense of Life." In *Bartlett's Familiar Quotations*, edited by Justin Kaplan, 631. 17th edition. Boston: Little, Brown, 2002.

Whitman, Walt. "Leaves of Grass." In *Bartlett's Familiar Quotations*, edited by Justin Kaplan, 519. 17th edition. Boston: Little, Brown, 2002.

Wikipedia. "Requiem for a Nun." https://en.wikipedia.org/wiki/Requiem_for_a_Nun.

Winthrop, John. "A Model of Christian Charity." In *Bartlett's Familiar Quotations*, edited by Justin Kaplan, 246. 17th edition. Boston: Little, Brown, 2002.

Yeats, William Butler. "Michael Robartes and the Dancer." In *Bartlett's Familiar Quotations*, edited by Justin Kaplan, 639. 17th edition. Boston: Little, Brown, 2002.